English on the Internet 1997–1998: A Student's Guide

Andrew T. Stull

Edited by
V.J. Benokraitis

Adapted for English Composition and Literature by
Emily Thiroux
California State University, Bakersfield

Prentice Hall, Upper Saddle River, NJ 07458

Copyright © 1998 by Prentice-Hall, Inc.
Simon & Schuster/A Viacom Company
Upper Saddle River, New Jersey 07458

Printed in the United States of America

All rights reserved. No part of this book may be reproduced or transmitted in any form or by any means, electronic or mechanical, including photocopying, recording, or any information storage and retrieval system, without permission in writing from the publisher.

10 9 8 7 6 5 4 3 2 1

ISBN 0-13-760588-9

TRADEMARK INFORMATION:
America Online is a registered trademark of Quantum Computer Services Incorporated;
CompuServe is a trademark of CompuServe, Incorporated;
Windows is a trademark of Microsoft Corporation;
Mosaic is a trademark of the National Center for Supercomputing Applications;
Navigator is a registered trademark of Netscape Communications Corporation;
Java is a registered trademark of Sun Microsystems.

The authors and publisher of this manual have used their best efforts in preparing this book. The authors and publisher make no warranty of any kind, expressed or implied, with regard to these programs or the documentation contained in this book. The author and publisher shall not be liable in any event for incidental or consequential damages in connection with, or arising out of, the furnishing, performance, or use of the programs described in this book.

Contents

Preface   Change!   v

Introduction   O' Brave New World: Brief Internet History   1

Chapter 1   What Makes It Tick? The Basics   4

                 1.1   Springs, wheels, and dials—Connecting   4
                 1.2   Putting the pieces together—Organizing   9
                 Activity: *The Starting Line*   11

Chapter 2   Hitting the Road: Mapping the Net   13

                 2.1   Cruising the net—Browsing   13
                 2.2   Landmarks—Navigating   137
                 2.3   Asking for directions—Searching   22
                 Activity: *The Great Cybertrip*   25

Chapter 3   Traveling in Style: As You Like It   27

                 3.1   Coffee, tea, or milk?—Customizing   27
                 3.2   Wish you were here—Communicating   32
                 3.3   The fun is in the going—Extending   41
                 Activity: *A Talkabout Tour*   44

Chapter 4   Back to the Future: Advanced Techniques   45

    4.1   There's no place like home—Designing   45
    4.2   Opening your own shop—Serving   57
    Activity: *Show that You've Arrived*   60

Appendix

    I   Stepping Out: Student Homepage Template   63
    II Sock It to Me: Internet Resources for English Composition and Literature   67
    III Documenting Your Electronic Sources   83
    IV Netiquette   91

Glossary   Fasten Your Seatbelts: Supercalifragilistics   97

Preface
Change!

The artist picks up the message of cultural and technological challenge decades before its transforming impact occurs.*

Change! The original edition of this manual gasped its first breath at 7:22 P.M. on July 23, 1995. It is now 2:04 P.M. on January 31, 1997 and a great deal about the World Wide Web and the world at large has changed. Dealing with change is a basic requirement for surviving in our modern world, and anticipating change may even make you rich. Our world is louder, faster, and more complex than the ones experienced by earlier generations. In terms of information transfer, we might be described as a techno-generation; our parents, as a paper-generation. In the past year and a half, the World Wide Web changed at an extraordinary rate, and it will probably continue to do so; our on-line future is likely to be chaotic but exciting. Prepare to revel in the difference that tomorrow will bring.

Reading this manual won't teach you all there is to know about the World Wide Web, but it will help you to teach yourself. In the future you will need to find information for yourself rather than relying solely on others, who may bear outdated knowledge. If you are successful, your skills in "cruising" the Internet will allow you to deal with perpetual change. By the end of this manual, you should be comfortable and resourceful in navigating the complexity of the Internet, from its back eddies to its thriving thoroughfares.

This manual has four chapters. In the Introduction, O' Brave New World, we will describe the origin of and the innovations behind the Internet. In Chapter One, What Makes It Tick?, we will explain the use of a Web browser and describe how you can obtain a connection to the

---

*After each major heading, you'll see a quote from Understanding Media, The Extensions of Man (MIT Press, Cambridge, MA, 1964) byMarshall McLuhan. See also "McLuhan Meets the Net," by Larry Press, Communications of the ACM, July 1995.

Internet. The boxed and end-of-chapter exercises will give you practice in using your browser, as well as expose you to some of the wonderful places on the Internet.

In Chapter Two, Hitting the Road, you'll learn more about how to use your browser in order to cruise the endless byways of the Internet. Also, you will be introduced to resources and strategies for information searching. The boxed and end-of-chapter exercises will reinforce your navigational skills and give you practice in searching for some of the great resources available to you on the Internet. In particular, we will cover resources for English Composition and Literature. These resources, along with related newsgroups, appear in Appendix II.

In Chapter Three, Traveling in Style, you will learn about how to fine customize your Web browser to make it more responsive to your needs. Also, you will find yourself changing from an observer into an enthusiastic Internet participant. The boxed and end-of-chapter exercises will help you reach out and make contact with others on the Internet.

In Chapter Four, Back to the Future, you will move into the fast lane of Web publishing. We'll discuss the ins and outs of Web design, HTML editing software, and Web server development.

In addition to the Internet resources listed in Appendix II, a student homepage template is provided in Appendix I. Finally, a glossary defines the buzzwords.

Acknowledgments

I'd like to thank Joe Thornton for his invaluable help, expertise, and guidance. His generosity with his knowledge and skill make it possible for me to accomplish my goals.

I would also like to thank Maggie Barbieri and Liz Kendall of Prentice Hall for the opportunity to do this project.

Emily Thiroux

Introduction
O' Brave New World
Brief Internet History

As electrically constructed, the globe is no more than a village.

This thing that we now call the Internet has been evolving ever since it was first developed over twenty-five years ago. Many people have compared the Internet to a living creature because of the way it grows and changes. You may find its history quite interesting. Also, the reasons for its creation and growth are helpful in understanding the nature, terminology, and culture of the people who have adopted the Internet as home.

In the late 50s and early 60s, scientists and engineers realized the importance of sharing information and communicating through their computers. Many different groups attempted to develop computer network languages that would enable computers to exchange information with one another. Most were successful. But ironically, all of these computer systems used different languages—people on different systems still had difficulty communicating with one another. It was like the Tower of Babel all over again.

The Internet was born as the solution to this problem. The U.S. government paid for the development of a common network language, called a *protocol*. which was eventually shared freely. Over time, many formerly isolated networks from all over the world adopted this language. Thus, the best description of the Internet is that it is not a network, but a network of networks. However, the Internet is independent of governments and regulation—there is no central Internet agency. Change is spurred by the common needs of the people that use the Internet.

Admittedly, this type of network system isn't the most graceful—but it works. If you saw a diagram of this great big computer network, you might find it resembles a spider's web. On this web, information can travel between any two points along any one of many possible paths.

Originally, the chief purpose of the Internet was to provide a distribution system for scientific exchange and research. Gradually, however, the Internet also became a digital post office, enabling people to send mail and transfer computer files electronically. Although the Internet is still used extensively by scientists, the commercial sector is currently the most powerful force behind its growth.

Historically, as technology changed, the speed with which information could be transferred and the way we viewed information changed. In 1991, an important new user interface was developed at the University of Minnesota: the *Gopher*. *Gopher* is a visually-oriented search tool for the Internet that allows users to locate information found on other computers. Because of *Gopher*, and other, more sophisticated *graphical user interfaces* developed since 1991, it is now possible to search through vast stores of information on computers all over the world. Once the desired information is found, it can be easily downloaded to the user's computer. Amazing if you think about it! You could be on your computer in Shepherdstown, West Virginia, and view information from London, Mexico City; or Tokyo without even realizing it. Wham! And no airline tickets!

In 1992, researchers in Switzerland helped to create a new format for information exchange that led to the explosive growth of the World Wide Web (WWW). Information on the Web is posted as a "page" that may contain text, images, sounds, and even movies. The organization of a page is much like any printed page in a book. However, Web pages make use of *hypermedia*. Hypermedia involves the use of words and images as links, or connecting points, between different texts, images, sounds, or movies on other computers throughout the world. *Hypertext* Web pages contain links only to other text documents.

However, the introduction of the Web created a dilemma: It was a great place to go, but there was no easy way to get there (kind of like the moon in the 60s.) We still lacked a convenient software program that would allow users to access the Web easily. In 1993, a program called *Mosaic* was developed by the National Center for Supercomputing Applications (NCSA). It allowed the user to browse Web pages as well as use other Internet resources such as electronic mail (e-mail).

After this browser was released, the Web has begun to grow faster than the speed of light. In 1991, around 700,000 people were using the Internet. After *Mosaic* came out, users increased to around 1.7 million. The release of another innovative browser, Netscape *Navigator*, took place when users were estimated at 3.2 million (July 1994). Since then, the growth hasn't slowed much—various estimates suggest that the number of people who have access to the Internet ranges from 20 million to 100 million.

Today the Internet is changing at staggering rates and becoming more readily available to the average person. Just listen to the computer jargon in the popular media. When was the last time you saw a television program, heard a radio commercial, or read a magazine without encountering something about the Internet?

Today, you have access to animation, video clips, audio files, and even virtual reality worlds. Imagine all the new ways we will be able to view tomorrow's digital world.

For those of you who already have some Web experience, here are a few Web addresses discussing the history and growth of the Internet. Simply type the address into your Web browser exactly as it appears below. If you are just beginning to learn about the Internet, you might want to visit these sites after you learn more about Web browsers and Internet addresses in Chapter Two.

BBN Timeline
BBN includes an Internet history timeline. It places the important Internet events in context with other historical events and throws in plenty of social commentary to give you perspective.
Address: http://www.bbn.com/customer_connection/timeline.htm

Hobbes' Internet Timeline
Hobbes' site offers a great deal about the Internet, the people who use it, and online culture.
Address: http://info.isoc.org/guest/zakon/Internet/History/HIT.html

Netizens: On the History and Impact of Usenet and the Internet
This is a comprehensive collection of essays about the history, nature, and impact of the Internet.
Address: http://www.columbia.edu/~hauben/netbook/

Chapter 1
What Makes It Tick?
The Basics

*An Indian is the servomechanism of his canoe,
as the cowboy of his horse or the executive of his clock.*

Many of you reading this manual have a lot of experience with computers, while others have little or none. In the first section of this chapter, we will briefly describe the basic computer setup you will need, how to use a modem, and choose an Internet Service Provider (ISP). Many of you may have computers on your campus that are set up to allow Internet access. In case you do not, we will list the minimum in terms of systems, connections, and services that you will need for the Internet. There are a staggering number of computers, software, and connections that you can use to get onto the Internet.

In the second section of this chapter, we will explain some of the idiosyncrasies of the Internet and describe the general features of most Internet browser software. A popular Web browser, Netscape *Navigator*, is used to illustrate discussions. Another popular browser is *Internet Explorer* from Microsoft. Both are *free* to students. We do not advocate any particular browser; you will probably want to try various browsers and make up your own mind. Although our illustrations focus on *Navigator*, fear not; both browsers share many of the same features. Once you have learned the basic techniques, it is easy to switch back and forth.

Section 1.1
Springs, wheels, and dials—Connecting

What is the difference between a Rolex and a Timex? Okay, it might seem like a silly question, but give it some consideration. The main difference is the price. But if we consider how well each of these watches meets our basic need for being on time, the two watches are very similar. The same goes for computers and networks. The simple no-frills components will save you money; the high-gloss gear will transform your cash into dash and make your Internet browsing only a little more enjoyable.

To get started, you will need a *computer*, a *modem*, an *Internet connection*, and *browser software*. The descriptions that follow will help you understand each component and its function to access the Internet.

The Computer

Be careful how you approach this issue if you ask someone for advice on which computer to buy. Many people have strong opinions about the differences between Macintosh and PC-compatible systems. The best advice that we can give to you is to test them both at a computer store. Choose the one that you can pay for and are most comfortable using.

These are the minimum system configurations that you will need:

Macintosh
- 68030
- System 7.0
- 256 color monitor
- 16 MB of RAM
- 8 MB of free disk space for browser software

PC-Compatible
- Intel 486
- Windows 3.1
- VGA monitor
- 16 MB of RAM
- 8 MB of free disk space for browser software

A new innovation is the Network Computer, or NC. An NC is a computer without all of the things that you would expect in an ordinary computer: word processing, drawing, graphing, and number crunching. Because these features may be helpful to you, you should consider the purchase of an NC carefully. An NC (a box that sits on top of your TV) will allow you to connect your television directly to the Internet. *WebTV* is currently the most popular, but we suspect that you will see many different brands in the future. The advantage of such products is that they are much cheaper than an ordinary (but more capable) computer. Also, you do not have to be a computer whiz to use them.

The Modem

You probably want to know why you need a modem if you already have a computer. A modem is a device that MOdulates and DEModulates—that is, it translates a computer signal into a telephone signal, and vice versa. Although computers and telephones were set up to speak different "languages," you can use a modem to translate between your computer and another computer across your telephone line. Modems come in different "sizes," so do not just go out and buy the cheapest one on sale. Definitely do not buy one from a garage sale unless you really know what you are doing. Because modem technology changes so quickly, older equipment may be useful only as a doorstop. The number one thing that you need to know about a modem is its speed of transmission. Modem speeds are referred to in units called baud (a bit is a basic unit of digital information and a baud is the speed of transmitting 1 bit in 1 second). At one time a modem speed of 2600 baud was considered adequate. However, the minimum speed requirements have been steadily increasing as users demand more information at faster rates. You should purchase a modem with a speed of at least 28,800 baud (28.8K baud). With a typical 28.8K baud modem you can expect that it will take a few seconds to transfer a typical Web page. However, keep in mind that manufacturers will continue to introduce newer and faster modems as pages become more complex and slower to load, and as users demand faster speeds.

You also need to make sure that your modem will work with your computer's operating system. Generally, this is not a big deal, as all modems are basically the same and top manufacturers produce software for all of the major operating systems. Just remember to read the box to make sure it contains the software you need. Included with the software is an installation manual and a phone number to a help desk. If you run into trouble, do not hesitate to try both. As for which brand of modem to purchase, buy what you can afford. Your Internet Service Provider or your campus computer administrator may recommend a particular brand of modem. Take this suggestion seriously. The technicians within your ISP or campus are likely to be familiar with the recommended modem and will be able to help you if problems arise.

The word *modem* may also refer to a device that allows you to connect your computer or television to a service line. By the time this guide is published, you will undoubtedly hear of things called ISDN modems and cable modems. An ISDN modem is a classic misnomer because the ISDN signal is already understood by computers and is not modulated and does not need to be demodulated. The cable modem refers to a box that connects between your cable TV line (not your telephone line) and your computer or television.

The Internet Connection

Your campus may already be using the Internet as a teaching and learning tool. If not, many resources exist to help you set up a connection from home.

Some campuses, although lacking a walk-in lab, have made arrangements for students to dial into the campus computer system and connect to the Internet with a modem. If this is the case, then search out the campus computer guru and ask for help.

Another option is to subscribe to a company such as *America Online*, *CompuServe*, *Prodigy*, *Microsoft Network*, or one of the many independent Mom and Pop companies currently offering monthly access to the Internet. It is a buyer's market and you should shop around. Test drive everything before you buy. This will save you a great deal of frustration. Here are a few things to consider when choosing an Internet Service Provider:

> ***Does the ISP have a local number for your area?*** You need to call the provider each time you access the Internet. Paying a toll call every time you do so will cost you a ton of money if you use the Internet regularly.
> ***Can their system handle a large number of simultaneous connections?*** Ask them how many users they can handle at one time and how many subscribers they have. Although they may have a reasonable price and a local number, it does not mean much if you can not get on to use it. If after you subscribe you find that you are never able to connect or that the only available access is late at night or early in the morning, then find a new ISP.
> ***Do they offer SLIP/PPP connections?*** This is the type of connection that you will need if you want to use a graphical browser like *Navigator* or *Internet Explorer*. Some ISPs only offer shell accounts. Shell accounts require you to type in each command as you would with a command-line interface such as provided in DOS. It is somewhat like driving a horse and buggy when everyone else has an automobile.
> ***Do they have a reasonable monthly subscription fee?*** Cheapest is not always best. The added features and the staffing support are important points to consider when choosing a service. Some Internet Service Providers offer you unlimited monthly connect time at a

flat fee and others offer you a per hour fee with additional hours costing extra. You will need to estimate your expected usage and purchase accordingly. Ask if there is a fee to upgrade your service if you find that you need more time. If you have a roommate, then consider upgrading the service and splitting the cost. This may save you money.

Does your ISP include the Internet browser software in the price? You will find that not all do. Most ISPs have an agreement with either Netscape or Microsoft to bundle their browser software. The provided software may also be partially configured to work on the ISP's system. Moreover, the technicians will be better able to help you with a problem.

Is the ISP a regional or local company? This may not be important to everyone, but some of you may go home during holidays and vacation. If the ISP covers a wider area, then you can still check your e-mail and cruise the Net when you are away from school.

Do they have a help line in case you need technical assistance to set up your connection? Call the help line before you subscribe and make sure you get a real person. Although you may be asked to leave your name and number, you should expect to get a return call within 24 hours. If they do not return your call within this time period, then the service is probably understaffed or poorly managed.

Does the ISP offer both newsgroup and e-mail access in addition to a connection to the Web? This is usually standard but there are always exceptions; it is better to ask up front.

Does it cost you extra for additional e-mail addresses? If you have a roommate, then you may find that it is more affordable to split the cost of a subscription and pay for an additional e-mail account.

Will your ISP add newsgroups at your request? Most ISPs subscribe to a small fraction of the available newsgroups and you may find that they do not include some of the basic, academic groups that your instructors may recommend. It should not cost anything for the ISP to add these groups to their list.

Does the ISP offer you space for your own Web page? Often, one of the features offered in the basic package is the option of constructing and posting your own homepage. The ISP usually sets a memory usage limit that affects the total size of the page and its traffic flow (that is, the number of people viewing the site).

The most important thing to remember when using an ISP is to expect courteous and prompt service. If you do not like what you are paying for, then cancel and go somewhere else. There are plenty of competitors willing to offer you better service.

The Browser Software

A descriptive name for software such as *Navigator* or *Internet Explorer* is *browser* software, because that is what most people do with it. It is used to browse or wander, sometimes aimlessly, through the Internet.

Many Web browsers are on the market today, and new ones frequently enter the race to capture your dollar.

All browsers have advantages and disadvantages. You should evaluate several and choose the one that is most comfortable for you. (However, when choosing a browser, remember that seeing over the dashboard is all that is really important. Do not get wrapped up in features that you will never use.) *Navigator, Internet Explorer,* and many of the other browsers are FREE for student use! Do not be afraid to look at several. At the end of the chapter you will find several Web addresses that offer such software. Of course, if you purchase the browser at the store, you also get a user's manual, which you do not get with the free, educational copy.

If you have all of these basic elements and they have been put together correctly, you should be ready to surf. (See the activity at the end of this chapter, The Starting Line.) The rest of this manual is devoted to guiding you through some of the many strange and wonderful places that will allow you to enjoy the depth and uniqueness of English Composition and Literature.

Section 1.2
Putting the pieces together—Organizing

The software that you will use to access the Net is commonly called a *Client* or a Web *browser*. It functions according to an information exchange model called the *Client-Server model* (Figure 1.1). In this way, a client (your Web browser software) communicates with a server (a computer with Web server software) on the Internet to exchange information. When referring to the Web, the information that your browser receives from the server is called a *page*.

What really appears on these Web pages? The best way to find out is to see for yourself. Sit down in front of a computer, start your browser software, and connect to the Internet. Your browser is probably already set to start at a specific page. This start page is often referred to as a *homepage*. Web pages usually include both text and images. Some also use sounds and videos. The use of different information types is called multimedia. A basic

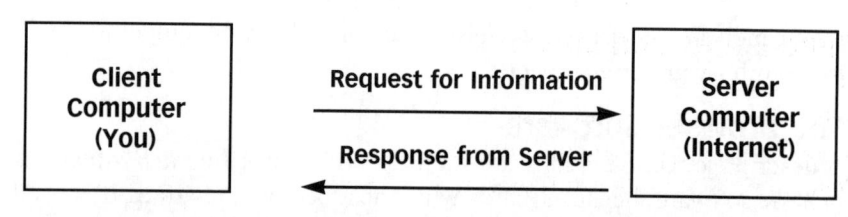

```
┌─────────────┐   Request for Information   ┌─────────────┐
│   Client    │ ──────────────────────────▶ │   Server    │
│  Computer   │                             │  Computer   │
│   (You)     │ ◀────────────────────────── │ (Internet)  │
└─────────────┘    Response from Server     └─────────────┘
```

Figure 1.1 The Client requests information from the server. The requested information is displayed on the client computer.

rule of the road is that anything that can be saved or recorded onto a computer can be distributed on the Internet through a Web page.

When you choose a page it will be sent to your computer. After the requested information has been sent by the server, your computer will display it for you. However, sometimes the Internet is not as responsive as you would like. (Why do you think some people refer to the World Wide Web as the World Wide Wait?) A few analogies and real-world considerations may help you see why this is so.

Patchwork Quilts

The patchwork quilt you might use during cold nights is one analogy. The quilt may have been crafted together by your grandmother. Or in another time, a community of women (not all with equal sewing talent) may have met to produce a single quilt from a collection of patches differing in color, shape, and pattern. Due to the complexity, age, use, care, and variations in craftsmanship, quilts eventually become threadbare and require mending. The Internet is just like your favorite quilt in this respect.

Spider Webs

As we mentioned in the introduction, the Internet can be thought of as a big spider web. If you are the spider and you are trying to get to a fly stuck in the web, you usually have more than one path to get there. Some paths are more direct than others, but there are choices. Like a spider web, sometimes a small section of the Internet drops out of the "Web" and traffic has to be rerouted. This obviously causes increased traffic on the remaining strands, which in turn increases your waiting time.

Far Away Places

Remember that the Internet mimics the real world. Distance is a factor in determining how long it takes to access a Web page. Generally, loading a page from a machine across town is much faster than loading a page from across the nation or across the world.

Time Zones and Lunch

The world works on different time zones and the Internet does too. And what about lunch? Most people in the Western world take lunch around noon, and a many of them check their e-mail or browse the Web as well. You can usually expect Internet traffic to be slow during that time. Let's now consider the distance factor. There is a three-hour time difference between the East and West coasts of North America, so the lunch rush lasts about four hours. Your location will determine if you are on the lead, middle, or tail end of the rush. Plan accordingly.

Parking Lots

Surfing the Web can be like shopping during the holidays. You either arrive early or park a few miles away. Here is the connection: A transaction occurs between your computer and another when you load a Web page for viewing. You require a document (a Web page) from somewhere on the Internet (a server). Obviously, a slow connection to the Internet on the client side may cause delays. But consider what is happening on the server end of the transaction. Small, slow servers will take longer to serve Web pages than large, fast servers. Now think about the holiday rush: Although there is normally adequate parking, a holiday sale and a limited number of parking spaces can add hours to your shopping. It should not be difficult to see how large, fast servers can be rapidly overloaded if they are hosting a really interesting Web site.

When Microsoft released an updated version of *Internet Explorer*, over twenty state-of-the-art machines went down because of excessive demand. Basically, Microsoft's parking lot was not big enough for the shopping rush.

By this time, you probably understand enough about each of the basic components of an Internet-ready computer to make a start. Even if you are feeling unsure, do not worry. You do not need to know everything there is to know about each component. And you can always learn more from the user's guides provided by the manufacturers. Just take it one step at a time and you will piece everything together.

Activity
The Starting Line

There's no better time than now to get started. And you really don't need a destination to have fun. This activity is intended to help you get ready to cruise or surf the Internet. Even if you don't have a computer to access the Internet, use a friend's computer or one on campus to view this material.

The Browser

You should have a computer and a modem. Use the following Internet addresses to research the right browser for you.

> **Netscape**
> http://www.netscape.com
> **Microsoft**
> http://www.microsoft.com
> **Browserwatch**
> http://browserwatch.iworld.com

The Internet Service Provider

With your computer, modem, *and* browser, you're only one step away. Use the following Internet addresses to research the right ISP for you. You might want to consider the questions we outlined previously.

> **Choosing the Internet Service Provider (Netscape)**
> http://home.netscape.com/assist/isp_select/index.html
> **Internet Access Provider Guide**
> http://www.liii.com/~dhjordan/students/docs/welcome.htm
> **Choosing An Internet Provider**
> http://tcp.ca/Dec95/Commtalk_ToC.html
> **Internet Service Providers by Area Code**
> http://thelist.iworld.com

Research

It's always nice to have an independent opinion; therefore, read what the critics have to say. The following Internet addresses are for two of the largest publishers of computer-related magazines. Between them, they print nearly 50 different popular periodicals about computers and the Internet. Search their databases for articles that will help you make Internet decisions. You can read the articles online.

> **CMP Media** (Publisher of *Windows Magazine* and others)
> http://www.techweb.com/info/publications/publications.html
> **Ziff Davis** (Publisher of *PC Magazine*, *MacUser*, and others)
> http://www5.zdnet.com/findit/search.html

Chapter 2
Hitting the Road
Mapping the Net

> *Under electronic technology the entire business of man becomes learning and knowing.*

By now, you should be prepared to see the world, or at least the World Wide Web. In this chapter, you'll develop a better understanding of the browser as a tool for navigating the Internet. The first section discusses basic navigation techniques; the second describes how to read Internet addresses; and the third introduces you to some of the information tools available on the Internet for finding your way around.

Section 2.1
Cruising the Net—Browsing

Even though the Internet is vast, finding your way around is no harder then finding your way to a friend's house. Information on the Internet has an address just as your friends do. Most browsers allow you to type in an address and thereby access information, or "go to," a particular document.

Let's take a look at how to enter an address using the Web browser Netscape *Navigator*, shown in Figure 2.1. Start by finding the text entry box, which is located to the right of the words *GoTo*. (Sometimes the word *Location* is used instead.) If you have *Navigator*, type in the address and press the return button on your keyboard.

Now take a look at the row of boxes directly above the text box. Each one contains an icon; together, they are known as the *tool bar*. Clicking on an individual box causes the computer to execute the command noted within the box.

How do each of these commands help you to navigate the Internet? Let's return to our analogy. Suppose you go to a friend's new home for a party but forget the house-warming present. What do you do? Drive home, of course. A Web browser will let you do something similar. In Figure 2.1, find the button labeled *Back*—it's at the far left. By clicking on this button you can return to the Web page you just visited. If you have gone to many Web pages, you can use it repeatedly to make your way back to your starting point.

> Here's the address of a site you might want to visit. When you type it into your browser, you'll arrive at *NewsLinks*, which is published by Simon and Schuster. It's not free but it is very reasonable and very good.
>
> **http://www.ssnewslink.com/**
>
> *NewsLink* is a subscription service that you can use to get news delivered about current issues and events. Among others, The Associated Press and *US News and World Report* provide free news services. You can reach them at the following addresses:
>
> **http://www.csmonitor.com/headlines/apfeed/apfeed.html**
> **http://www.usnews.com/**

Now find the *Home* button. By selecting this button, you will immediately return to the homepage configured for your browser. When you first begin using your browser, it will be set to a page determined by the company that created it. Later on, you'll learn how to make any page you wish into a homepage, and even to create your own. But for now, remember that you can always go home.

Two other buttons common to most browsers are *Stop* and *Reload*. *Stop* is pretty easy to understand but *Reload* needs just a bit more expla-

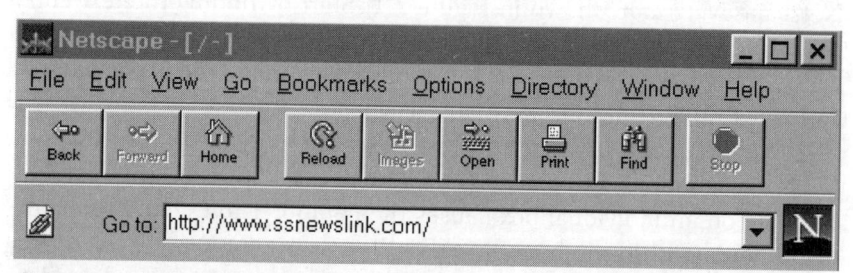

Figure 2.1. The tool bar for Netscape *Navigator* offers basic navigation features such as *Back*, *Forward*, and *Home*. You will find everything you'll need to navigate around the Internet.

nation. As you explore more of the Internet, you'll realize that complete pages don't show up in your browser window instantly. Instead, different types of elements (pictures, icons, text, animations, etc.) appear over time as they are moved from the server to your browser. Occasionally, you'll notice that a page loads without some of these elements. This is often caused by an error in the transmission. Use the Reload button to request a new copy of the page.

You don't always have to know the address of a page to view it. The wonderful thing about the Web is that you can access pages through the use of *hyperlinks*. You will notice that hyperlinks are often colored words (typically blue) on a Web page. Images may also be hyperlinks. Your mouse is used to select or click on the desired hyperlink. Some Web authors write their pages so that their hyperlinks are hidden from you. If you aren't sure where the hyperlinks are, just click on everything. You can't break anything. Clicking on a hyperlink will take you to a new Web page just as typing in an address does.

Here are a few more places you might find both fun and interesting.

The Academy of American Poets
http://www.he.net/~susannah/academy.htm

The Shakespeare Web
http://www.shakespeare.com/

Writing Essays
http://www.english.upenn.edu/~jlynch/writing.html

Writing Research Papers
http://falcon.eku.edu/honors/beyond-mla/#MLA-help

Inkspot
http://www.inkspot.com

Macarena Lessons
http://www.nsmi.com/macarena

Resume Software
http://www.decisivequest.com

Use this opportunity to experiment with each of the toolbar buttons on your browser. Remember that you can always use your *Back*, *Forward*, or *Home* buttons to retrace your steps.

The author of a Web page can connect one image to *many* different places. This type of hyperlink is sometimes called a *clickable map*. For example, think of a Web page with a map of a recent archaeological dig. The creator of such a document could place a hyperlink at various locations on the map so that your selection of these locations would take you to different information about the artifacts that were found there. For a little experience in using this type of navigation, visit the sites in the following box.

> Here are three addresses that use clickable maps. They are also great places to find helpful information.
>
> **Atlantic Unbound: Books and Authors**
>   http://www.theatlantic.com/atlantic/atlweb/bookauth/baindex.htm
>
> **Poets in Person**
>   http://www.wilmington.net/arts/poets/
>
> **Bookwire**
>   http://www.bookwire.com/homepage.html
>
> Not all browsers support clickable maps. However, most good Web authors will provide conventional hyperlinks to related sites in addition to the clickable map.

Some Web pages contain *forms*. A form is generally a request for information, which you may respond to by clicking with your mouse or typing an answer. Forms can be used to survey users, answer questions, or make requests. As the box below shows, you can obtain valuable information from companies, government agencies, or educational institutions.

> Experiment with the following links which involve forms. Not all browsers support forms, so you will need to determine if yours does.
>
>   http://www2.cruzio.com/~abbyb/
>   http://www.interlog.com/~ohi/inkspot/feedback.html
>   http://www.lsa.umich.edu/ecb/OWL/owl.html
>   http://www.census.gov/cdrom/lookup/

Section 2.2
Landmarks—Navigating

The Internet addresses that you've been using are also called *Uniform Resource Locators*, or *URLs*. Each URL (pronounced "earl") has a couple of basic parts just like a residential address. Look at some of the URLs that you've used already. Do you notice any similarities among them?

Here is another typical URL (this will take you to a pretty cool site). The three basic components of an URL are listed below the address. Compare this one to the others you've seen so far.

http://www.riddler.com/bridges/genericbr.html

protocol	http://
server	www.riddler.com
path	/bridges/genericbr.html

You may notice that some addresses don't have a path element—this information is not always necessary. Be careful when you type an URL. Even one incorrect letter will prevent the browser from finding the desired site. Here is an additional resource if you'd like to learn more about Internet addresses:

http://www.ncsa.uiuc.edu/demoweb/url-primer.html

Now pick up any recent magazine and leaf through the articles and advertisements. With little effort you should be able to recognize a few more URLs. Just as you might recognize a string of numbers to be a phone number (e.g., 555-1212), you should be able to spot URLs by their characteristic form and order. An URL may seem confusing at first glance, but think of it as a postal address strung together without any spaces.

The *protocol* of the URL indicates how the information is stored. In the last box, *http* refers to the protocol, or language, that is used by all Web servers. The colon and slashes are used to separate it from the name of the server. They are not necessarily present in every type of URL. The *path* describes the location of the Web page on the server.

> Up to this point, we have only been discussing browsers as a way of navigating through information using hyperlinks. However, browsers also have the power to link to other, much older, formats of information. Try the following URLs to notice how the information differs.
>
> ### ftp://sri.com/netinfo/interest-groups.txt
> ### gopher://gopher.marvel.loc.gov/
>
> HTTP, FTP, and Gopher are not the only protocols, but they are the three you're most likely to encounter. Have you ever encountered the following Internet protocols?
>
> **telnet://**
>
> **wais://**
>
> **news:**

A *domain* is just a fancy name for a functional network group. The last part of the server name defines the domain to which the server belongs. The most common domain is indicated by the letters *edu*; all educational institutions are members of this domain group. Another important domain is *com*, which stands for commercial and includes Internet servers that belong to *commercial* companies. You are also likely to encounter domains that serve other groups; abbreviations for a few of these are shown below.

> Here are some URLs that may help expand your understanding of domains. Can you determine what each domain group represents?
>
> ### http://www.webaholics.com
> ### http://arts.endow.gov/
> ### http://www.dtic.dla.mil
> ### http://www.writer.org/
> ### http://www.internic.net
> ### http://www.en.utexas.edu/
>
> The first address suggests that surfing can be addictive. Don't say we didn't warn you.

In your travels, you will eventually jump to a server that is outside your country. Much, but not all, of the information on these servers is in English. URLs of servers outside the U.S. have an additional section at the end of the server name. It is a two letter code that indicates the country. Here are just a few examples of the many you might find. (All the country codes are listed in **http://www.ics.uci.edu/pub/websoft/www-stat/country-codes.txt.**)

- .au   Australia
- .ca   Canada
- .ch   Switzerland
- .nl   Netherlands
- .pe   Peru
- .uk   United Kingdom

> Here is yet another opportunity to encounter new places on the Web. It is a directory that allows you to search for specific things. This group of tools is discussed later in the chapter, but you might want to play with it first.
>
> **Yahoo!**
>   http://www.yahoo.com
>
> Remember you won't break anything. If you get lost, you can always shut down the program, have lunch, and try again later!

Return Visit

Now that you've found so many really interesting pages, how do you find them again a day or a week later? Your browser provides a way to mark an intriguing site and quickly return to it. Netscape calls this feature *Bookmarks* (see Figure 2.2). By using such a feature, you can compile a list of pages you frequently visit. When you wish to return to one of these pages, you simply select it from the list by clicking on it with your mouse. You will jump directly to the site.

Here is an URL to get your collection started. Try this address: **http://www.hotwired.com**. It's a pretty interesting place: the online version of Wired Magazine. If you have Netscape, select *Add Bookmark* from the *Bookmarks* menu (see Figure 2.2). Later on, if you use your mouse to select the *Bookmarks* menu, you'll see that *Hotwired* is just a

Figure 2.2. As pages are added to this list they will appear at the bottom of this same pull-down menu.

jump away. You don't have to memorize the URL or haphazardly jump around until you find it again.

Now that you've got the hang of it, give the following URLs a try.

A Peak at the Purdue Online Writing Lab
http://owl.english.purdue.edu/live.html

Univerity of Missouri Online Writery
http://www.missouri.edu/~wleric/writery.html

Surf the Best Websites
http://www.pointcom.com/

Aaron's Gift
http://www.ianet.net/~cando/

Beginner's Arena for HTML
http://www.deltamedia.com/crest/lists/beginner/index.html

Writer's Block
http://www.niva.com/writblok/index.htm

RongoRongo
http://www.netaxs.com/~trance/rongo.html

Science Fiction
http://julmara.ce.chalmers.se/stefan/WWW/Cyberlinks/saifai.html

Women's Activewear (Virtual Reality with QuickTime)
http://www.gildamarx.com/

Feminist Science Fiction, Fantasy, and Utopia
http://www.uic.edu/~lauramd/sf/femsf.html

> **Bartlett's Familiar Quotations**
> http://www.columbia.edu/acis/bartleby/bartlett/
>
> **Electronic Postcards**
> http://postcards.www.media.mit.edu/postcards/
>
> **Performing Arts, People, and Related News**
> http://www.culturefinder.com/
>
> **Take a Humor Break**
> http://www.misty.com/laughweb/
>
> **Jumpstart Your Writing Career: Romance**
> http://www.nettrends.com/success/about.htm
>
> **Hyerizons: Hypertext Fiction**
> http://www.duke.edu/~mshumate/hyperfic.html
>
> **The Skeptic's Dictionary**
> http://wheel.ucdavis.edu/~btcarrol/skeptic/dictcont.html
>
> When you find something that you think is fun and interesting, save it or give the address to a friend.

As you begin to accumulate more sites on your list, you'll notice how cluttered and disorganized they can become. In addition to the ability to collect Web addresses, most browsers also allow you to organize them as you desire. Refer to Figure 2.2 and notice the menu option immediately below the *Add . . .* feature. This option, called *Go to Bookmarks*, allows you to organize your Web address list. When you select this option, a small window will open; in it you can move and manipulate your list of Web addresses.

Travel History

If you've been working along with your manual and browser at the same time, you've probably been to many places on the Web. If you want to move back and forth between your selections, you're probably using the *Forward* and *Back* buttons on the browser toolbar. But what do you do if you want to go back to someplace you've visited fifteen jumps ago? Do you press the *Back* button fifteen times? Well, it works, but it is a little slow. You might want to try a new feature: It allows you to jump rapidly to any of the places you've visited along your path of travel. In *Navigator*, select the *Go* menu. You'll see a list of all of the places you've visited on your journey. To jump to a site on the list, simply click/select the site with your mouse. With *Navigator*, you'll also find a similar feature called *History* under the *Windows* menu. By selecting *History*, you'll open a new window listing the names *and* the URLs for all of the places you've visited recently. Other browsers have similar features.

Because the list compiled under *Go* or *History* begin anew each time you start your browser, you should use *Bookmarks* when you find something interesting.

Section 2.3
Asking for directions—Searching

The Internet is full of valuable information, but it's not always easy to find what you need. A number of easy-to-use tools are available for free. With practice, these tools will help you develop better information-finding skills.

There are two types of tools that you'll use most often to search for information. These are *Directories* and *Search Engines*.

Directories

Yahoo! (**http://www.yahoo.com**) is only one of many directories that are available on the Internet, but it is the best one available for general topics. (The name Yahoo is taken from Jonathan Swift's *Gulliver's Travels*, which describes a Yahoo as a crude, uncivilized, and according to one of *Yahoo's* founders, an interesting person.)

Yahoo! began as a simple listing of information by category, kind of like a card catalog. In the last two years, it has added the ability to search for specific information. At the top level of the directory, there are several very general categories, but as you move deeper into the directory you'll notice that the categories become more specific. To find information, you simply choose the most appropriate category at the top level and continue through each successive level until you find what you're looking for (or until you realize you're in the wrong place). It's not unusual to get lost. In such cases, just begin again and try different categories.

Suppose that you are interested learning more about reading and writing hypertext. What does *Yahoo!* have to say about this topic? Taking the tack that hypertext is a form of literature, we find that *literature* is listed in three of the seven categories Yahoo! shows with hypertext sections. Some of these seven categories also have terms such as *arts*, *humanities, computers,* and *World Wide Web* in common. Because *Yahoo!* cross-references among the categories, you'll find that several related categories will lead to the information you desire.

Much of your success in finding information with this type of tool really centers around your preparation for the search. Often, it is possible to find information on a topic in a category that may at first seem unrelated to your topic of interest. Again, let's take the example of hypertext. Are you especially interested in electronic literature? If so, you might search under the *Yahoo!* subcategory of *Electronic Literature.* (In *Yahoo!*, *Electronic Literature* is a subcategory of *Humanities,* which in turn is a subcategory of the top-level *Arts* category). In the category *Hypertext,* try the links provided in the *Computers and Internet* subcategory. Voila!

Prepare yourself for a search *before* you jump into one. In the long run, it will save you both time and frustration. Don't be afraid to try some unusual approaches in your search strategy. A good technique is to pull out your thesaurus and look up other names for the topic you're searching. Think of everything associated with your question and give each of these possibilities a try. You never know what might turn up a gold mine.

Search Engines

A more direct approach to finding information on the Web is to use a *search engine,* which is a program that runs a search while you wait for the results. Many search engines can be found on the Web. Some of Web search engines are commercial and may charge you a fee to run a search. Search engines are also available for other parts of the Internet: *Archie, Veronica,* and *Jughead* are examples of such search engines.

Alta Vista (**http://www.altavista.digital.com**) offers general and detailed searches through what Digital Equipment Corporation claims is the largest Web index. According to Alta Vista, the user has access to nearly 11 billion words found in nearly 22 million Web pages. In addition, you can access a full-text index of more than 13,000 newsgroups.

Excite! (**http://www.excite.com**) is very versatile because it tracks down information by searching for concepts, not just keywords. Suppose, for example, that you're interested in poetry. *Excite!* can find such information even though the source presents the works of, say, John Milton or Percy Bysshe Shelley without ever using the word "poetry." It also provides you with a percentage of how close it "thinks" it came to providing pertinent information on your concept(s). *Excite!* also has such capabilities as finding a specific news article from newsgroups by a text search.

InfoSeek Guide (**http://guide.infoseek.com**) is a search/browse service that returns both search hits and a list of topics related to your search. With each search, you get the most relevant matches, related topics to explore, and current news and views from popular magazines, TV networks, and online experts. *InfoSeek Guide* also helps you find email addresses, stock quotes, company profiles, and other materials. Projected to be the biggest and fastest, *InfoSeek* recently released *Ultraseek* (**http://www.ultraseek.com**).

A frequently used search engine is *Lycos* (**http://www.lycos.com**). It's simple to operate but, as with any search tool, it takes practice and patience to master. Take the time now to connect to *Lycos*, and we'll take it for a test run. The instructions on the opening page will tell you almost everything you need to know. To search, enter a word into the white text entry box and press the submit button. *Lycos* will refer back to its database of information and return a page of hyperlinked resources containing the word you entered. When the query results come back to you, notice that they are hyperlinks to various sites on the Internet.

To see how a search engine works, use *irony and satire* as a topic for a search. Observe that you can set the number of responses that the engine will return to you. Did you also notice that some of your results didn't seem to apply to your topic? This is one of the downfalls of search engines. They are very fast, but they don't think—that is your job. A search using the term *irony and satire* is just as likely to turn up a link to Netiquette as a link to the literary terms. To perform an effective search, you will need to spend time before the search preparing a search strategy. When you do research using an automated tool like a search engine, you can expect many links to be unrelated to your topic of interest. However, with continued development in advanced computing, smarter agents will undoubtedly be developed.

One last comment on search engines: these tools don't directly search the Internet. They actually search a database that is derived from the Internet. Here is how it works. Initially, information robots (automated programming tools) sift and categorize information on the Internet and place it into a database. It is this database that is inspected when you use a search engine. Therefore, each search engine is only as effective as its cadre of robots that generate the database. Thus it is wise not to rely on just one search engine. Use several, because what one does not find, another might.

Here's a way to test the skills you've developed from your accumulated Internet experience. Using Yahoo! and Lycos (or any of the other search tools described in this chapter), find information on the Web related to the words and phrases given below. Compare the results with searches using the additional resources provided at the bottom of this box. The last two resources allow you to choose from a collection of search tools.

Short Stories	**Gothic literature**
Censorship	**Online Writing Labs (OWLs)**
Viruses	**Freedom of Speech**
Hypertext	**Intellectual Property Rights**
Cyberspace	**Romanticism**

WebCrawler
  http://www.webcrawler.com

BigFoot
  http://www.bigfoot.com

HotBot
  http://www.hotbot.com

Findspot
  http://www.findspot.com

Search.com
  http://www.search.com

Activity
The Great Cybertrip

Obtaining information on the Web is easy. The hard part is accessing the right information. But discovering the correct information is still exciting and interesting, not unlike getting lost and finding your way again in an unfamiliar city. The first list below contains terms used in English Composition and Literature. See what you can find on these topics. Can you associate the terms in the list according to the fields mentioned?

- Ode
- Satire
- Comma splice
- Parallelism

- Parody
- Limerick
- Sonnet
- Epithet
- Synthesis
- Paraphrase
- Hypermedia
- Netiquette

- Tragedy
- Gothic
- Poetic justice
- Deconstruction
- Feminist theory
- Linguistics
- Argumentation
- Exposition

Understanding English Composition and Literature often means learning about the women and men who have made significant contributions in their disciplines. Below is a short list of some players in the fields mentioned in the beginning of this activity. Some of them will be very easy to track down, whereas others will not. We hope you'll find both their perspectives and their lives interesting

Your assignment, should you choose to accept it, is to put together a brief history of American Literature based on the personalities listed below. Include also their important contributions. Before this directive self-destructs, you might also link these people to their respective disciplines. Of course, some of them may be categorized into multiple fields. If you'd really like a challenge, try to draw a thread of connection between each individual, no matter how thin or obscure. (Hint: To help you understand the challenge, you might want to search out the term *Concept Map*).

- Sylvia Plath
- Edgar Allan Poe
- J. D. Salinger
- Benjamin Franklin
- Alice Walker
- Mark Twain
- Emily Dickinson
- Thomas Paine
- Noah Webster
- Nathaniel Hawthorne
- Flannery O'Conner

- John Greenleaf Whittier
- John Steinbeck
- John Grisham
- Robert Frost
- ee cummings
- Truman Capote
- Henry James
- Edith Wharton
- Edna Saint Vincent Millay
- Arthur Miller
- Jane Smiley

Remember to use all of the resources at your disposal. Begin with *Yahoo!* and then move to the other search engines. Check the obscure as well as the popular resources. You are also welcome to read ahead to Chapter Three, which explains how to use e-mail and newsgroups. These resources may be helpful, too.

Chapter 3
Traveling in Style
As You Like It

We shape our tools and afterwards our tools shape us.

By now you have probably wandered and stumbled through some of the many fascinating resources offered on the Web. In this chapter we will cover additional techniques to help you make your Web experience more enjoyable and beneficial.

Section 3.1
Coffee, tea, or milk? Customizing

On the Internet, saving time is critical if you have to use a modem and an Internet Service Provider (ISP) to cruise the Net. If you know what your browser can and cannot do, and if you configure the options for your browser so that it is most efficient for you, you will save both time and money. Try the modifications described below as you read; also, feel free to jump to the information that is most important to you.

With *Navigator*, you have several ways to customize the appearance and behavior of your browser. These customizing features are known as *Options*. Descriptions for some of the *Options* follow, as well as the reasons you might want to change them. After you investigate *Options*, you'll be able to explore the other custom features on your own.

> Some of you may want a more detailed description of your Netscape browser. Netscape has included access to a detailed set of descriptions and instructions on its homepage. To access the Netscape *Navigator Handbook*, select *Help* from the menu bar and choose *Hand-*

> *book* from the menu list. This will connect you to Netscape's on-line handbook. Because this information is online and not held within your browser, you need an active Internet connection to use it. You can access this same information from the following URL:
>
> http://home.netscape.com/eng/mozilla/3.0/handbook/

Setting Options

Navigator lists common functions under the *Options* menu on the menu bar at the top of the window. Select Options and a pull-down window will appear (Figure 3.1). Notice that there are check marks by some of the options. Look at *Auto Load Images*, for example. When the check is present, images will be automatically loaded. If you select this option again, the check mark disappears and subsequently pages will load the text without the time-consuming images. Give it a try. *Navigator* lists only the basic options here. Experiment with the other basic options (each of these begin with *Show*) to see what they do.

Additional options can be accessed from one of the *Preference...* sub-menus. (You can see these at the top of the *Options* pull-down menu.) Once you've selected one of *Navigator's Preferences...* windows, you'll notice that the preferences are broken down into categories according to function (Figure 3.2). The different categories are listed at the top of the window; they look like tabs in a file folder. As we describe differ-

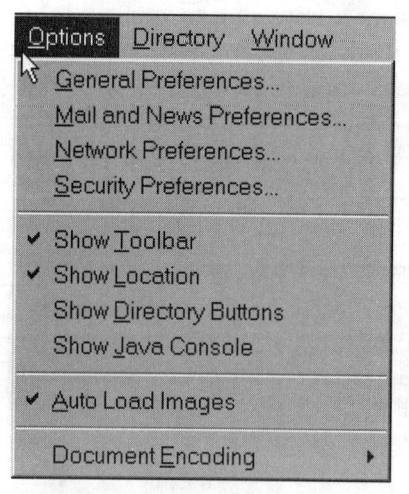

Figure 3.1. For Netscape *Navigator*, many of the general options are listed near the bottom of the *Options* menu. If you want to set specific options, you can select the different *Preferences...* available at the top of the box.

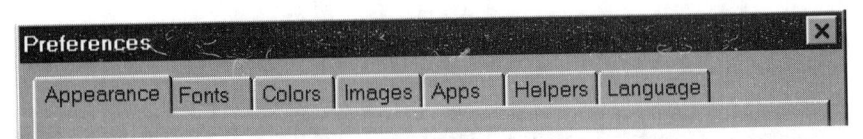

Figure 3.2. These are the *General Preferences* categories in *Navigator*. This illustration includes only the categories and not the contents of the window. The contents will vary depending on the tab selection. A different set of tabs and categories exist for each of the different *Preferences* windows.

ent customizing options, we will refer to both the specific preference window and the specific tab within that window (i.e., *General Preferences...* window and *Appearance* tab).

Now that you know where to go to modify the setup for your browser, we'll describe some of the features you may want to modify. You will probably want to look at each preference even if you choose not to modify it. Also, keep in mind that some of these changes are not relevant to your setup; others require specific information in order for your browser to work with your ISP. You can always check the online *Navigator Handbook* for help.

Homepage

You might want to modify the location of your homepage. A homepage is like "home base" in a game of hopscotch. It is the place you begin hopping from square to square. If you're working with a browser that hasn't been customized before, the company that made the browser probably chose the homepage. If you're working on one of your school's computers, then the homepage may already be set to the school's page. If you're permitted to change the homepage, then decide what you want to designate as your homepage. By now you've probably found something on the Web that you are willing to call home. When your homepage is properly set, every time you start your browser or select Home from the toolbar, you'll end up at this place. Later in this chapter, we'll discuss how you can make and display your own homepage.

In *Navigator*, open the *Options* menu, choose the *General Preferences* window and then select the *Appearance* tab. At the center of the window you will see a dialog box within the *Startup* control panel (Figure 3.3) that allows you to set your homepage. Type in the URL of your new homepage.

Linkage

You have probably noticed that hyperlinks are normally blue (unless someone has changed the default color). Once you've accessed the page that the

```
┌─ Startup ──────────────────────────────────────────────────┐
│  On Startup Launch:                                        │
│                    ☑ Netscape Browser  ☐ Netscape Mail  ☐ Netscape News │
│  Browser Starts With:  ○ Blank Page    ● Home Page Location: │
│                       ┌──────────────────────────┐         │
│                       │ http://www.home.com      │         │
│                       └──────────────────────────┘         │
└────────────────────────────────────────────────────────────┘
```

Figure 3.3. On *Navigator*, the *Startup* control panel within the *Appearance* tab of the *General Preferences* includes a dialog box that will allow you to enter the URL for your desired homepage.

hyperlink represents, it changes to purple. Think of this as the bread crumb principle. The purple links remind you that you've already been down a particular path (link) and that you might want to select a different path. Eventually, however, the hyperlink will change back to its default color. But you can designate the elapsed time before a hyperlink changes back to the default color. You can also choose the default color. Generally, the more time you spend on the Internet, the more quickly your links should revert to default (one day, say). If you travel frequently and find that your hyperlinks are always purple, then your expiration limit may be set too long.

From the *Options* menu, open the *General Preferences* window and select the *Appearance* tab. At the bottom of the window, you will see a dialog box that allows you to set the length of time in days for hyperlinks to expire (Figure 3.4).

Font Style, Size, and Color

If you spend a great deal of time on the computer, then you realize the importance of adjusting your monitor, desk, and keyboard to minimize potential eye strain and muscle fatigue. Selecting a font of appropriate color, style, and size should help alleviate the hazard.

To change the default style and size of the font, select the *Options* menu and open the *General Preferences* window. Select the *Font* tab from

```
┌─ Link Styles ──────────────────────────────────────────────┐
│  Links are:      ☑ Underlined                              │
│                                                            │
│  Followed Links: ○ Never Expire  ● Expire After: [1] Days  [Expire Now] │
└────────────────────────────────────────────────────────────┘
```

Figure 3.4. On *Navigator*, the *Link Styles* control panel within the *General Preferences* tab group allows you to control the appearance and behavior of hyperlinks.

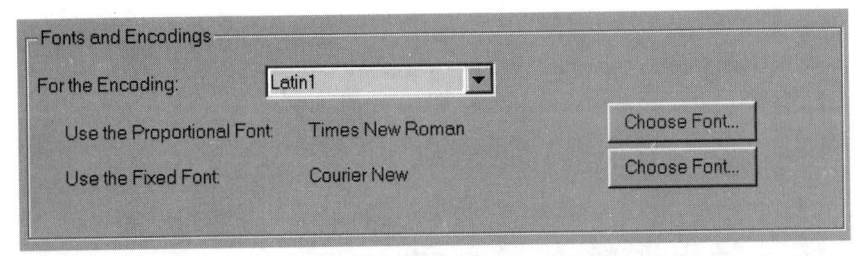

Figure 3.5. On *Navigator*, the *Fonts* tab group within the *General Preferences* option window allows you to choose the default font size and style of text elements.

this window (Figure 3.5). You may modify the default settings for both the font size and style used by your browser.

To view other possible font settings, select the appropriate *Choose Font...* button. You should work primarily with the proportional font setting because it is used for the normal text on your browser. (Fixed fonts are generally used when a page designer is illustrating computer code or text requiring uniform spacing.) A small window will appear; in it you can select from numerous font styles and sizes. When you click the *OK* button, those font settings will be selected as the default for your browser. If you like your selection, click the *OK* button at the bottom of the *Fonts* tab window.

To change the default colors, select the *Options* menu and open the *General Preferences* window. Select the *Colors* tab from this window (Figure 3.6). You may modify the default color settings used by your browser for the hyperlinks (*Links and Followed Links*) and regular text containing no hyperlinks (*Text*). (*Links* refer to unvisited links, whereas *Followed Links* refer to links already selected.)

To change the color setting, select the appropriate *Choose Color...* button. A small window will appear displaying numerous color choices. When you select the *OK* button, that color will be selected as your custom color. If you like your choice, then click the *OK* button in the *Colors* tab window.

Experiment with the *Colors* tab window a while. Try to modify both the text and background colors. Also, try to discover how you might use an image in the background instead of a solid color. Remember not to go overboard with your power; you still need to be able to read the words on the page. Some font colors or sizes may be difficult to read causing more eye strain.

Although we have not discussed all of the options, you probably have enough experience to understand how to use them. Experiment with the settings on your own. You can always check the online *Naviga-*

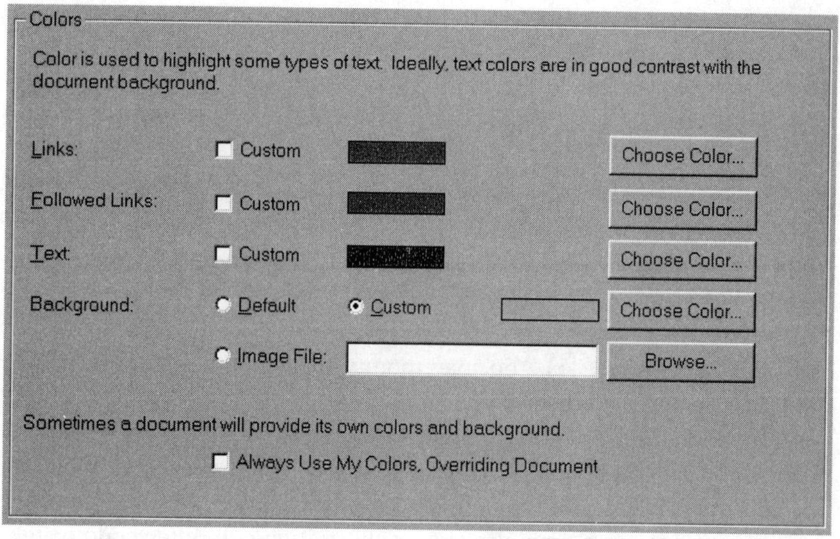

Figure 3.6. On *Navigator*, the *Colors* control panel within the *General Preferences* option group allows you to choose the default colors of hypertext and text elements.

tor *Handbook* for help. If you are using Microsoft *Internet Explorer* or another browser, you will find that they have very similar features.

Section 3.2
Wish you were here—Communicating

Navigator and most other browsers allow you to communicate through e-mail, newsgroups, and online interest groups. E-mail links are built into many Web pages and enable you to send correspondence directly to other people through the Internet.

E-mail

E-mail is the electronic exchange of mail among people. This exchange is from one person to one (or more) specified people. Like web browsers and web servers, e-mail operates according to a Client-Server model. Your client software asks a server computer for mail addressed to you. Your mail server is operated and maintained by the administrator of your campus or ISP. Although your Web server speaks a computer protocol called HyperText Transport Protocol (HTTP), your mail server speaks a computer protocol called Simple Mail Transport Protocol (SMTP).

Think of the server as your mailbox. The mailbox is where mail addressed to you is stored until you pick it up. You use your mail client to retrieve your mail from your mailbox.

Gaining access to an e-mail server is easy. If you are at a campus that has provided you with Internet access, you should be able to apply for an e-mail account through your campus computer administrator. Otherwise, you can apply for an e-mail account through an ISP. If you use an ISP to access to the Internet, you probably have e-mail capabilities. In order to properly configure your browser for sending e-mail, you need to know (1) your e-mail address and (2) the name of your mail server.

Before configuring the browser for e-mail, let's look at the form of an e-mail address: NAME@HOST.DOMAIN. It is not necessary to have a full name for the NAME part of the address; in fact, some addresses use only numbers to represent an individual.

Here are two typical e-mail addresses.

ethiroux@csubak.edu

joestage@aol.com

The three basic components of an e-mail address include

user name	ethiroux	joestage
host server	csubak	aol
domain	edu	com

Drop us a note if you have any comments about this manual.

Your *User Name* is also the NAME associated with your e-mail address. The @ symbol always follows the NAME and then the name of the server computer (HOST). The domain in the e-mail format, just like the domain of the URL format, is used to indicate the affiliation of the user. Notice that there are *no* spaces anywhere in an e-mail address. Sometimes dashes, periods, or underscores are used as separators in e-mail addresses. Also, e-mail addresses are not case sensitive, so you can capitalize letters at your discretion.

Your campus computer administrator or your ISP will provide you with an e-mail address. This is the address you'll give to your friends. It will also be posted with any correspondence you send on the Internet.

Configuring your browser to send and receive e-mail only takes two steps.

First: To set your personal information, select the *Options* menu and open the *Mail and News Preferences* window. Select the *Identity* tab and you will see the text entry boxes where you can enter your information (Figure 3.7).

Second: To set your e-mail information, select the *Options* menu and open the *Mail and News Preferences* window. Select the *Servers* tab and you will see the text entry boxes (Figure 3.8). After you've entered the correct information, restart the browser program. Now you should have the ability to send and receive e-mail. Think about it! You'll save on postage and long-distance phone bills.

Most e-mail systems use a single machine to handle both incoming and outgoing mail. However, some systems use a different machine for incoming and outgoing mail. In Figure 3.8, note that two different text entry boxes are provided for the mail server. If your system uses just one machine, enter the mail server twice. The person who sets up your account should be able to give you all the information you need. If they are less than helpful, then it is generally safe to assume that the address for both your incoming and outgoing mail server is MAIL.HOST.DOMAIN.

Now let's send some e-mail. Select the *Windows* option from the menu bar and choose *Netscape Mail*. A new window will open (Figure 3.9).

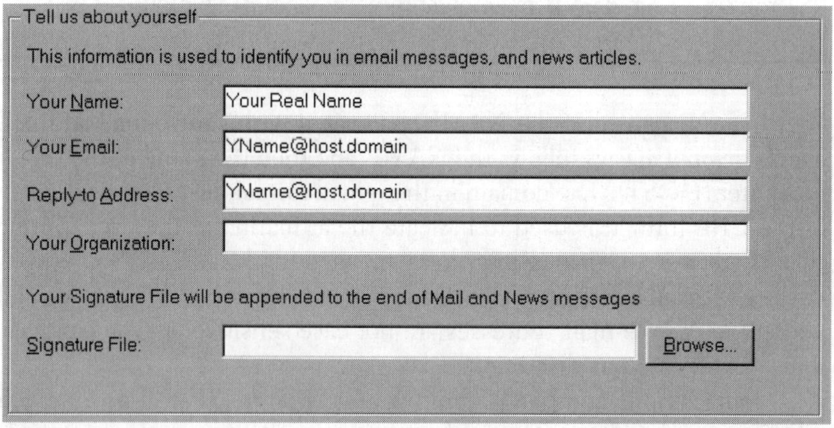

Figure 3.7. This information helps to identify you when you send e-mail. Use the Signature feature to place standard information (such as your address and phone number) at the bottom of your messages.

Figure 3.8. The information about your particular mail server and e-mail address must be entered before you can receive e-mail from others through *Navigator*.

Notice that this window is similar to a Web browser. (It is also similar to the news reader that we will discuss later.) To view your mail, select the *Get Mail* button. If you have mail, then it will appear on the left side of the window. All incoming mail arrives in the *Inbox*. When you select the *Inbox*, its contents will appear on the right side of the window. Finally, when you select a specific mail item you will see the contents displayed at the bottom of the window. To test the setup, send yourself an e-mail message. Next, write your congressperson. You can find her address in the box below.

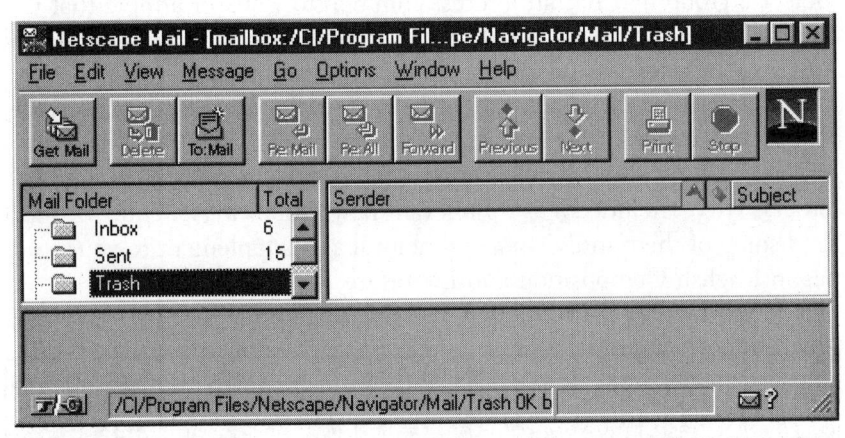

Figure 3.9. *Navigator* includes a built-in mail client. Its features are similar to those of a Web browser.

> Now that you've got the basics down, here are two sites you'll find useful.
>
> **A Beginner's Guide to Effective Email**
> http://www.webfoot.com/advice/email.top.html
>
> **Congressional E-mail Directory**
> http://www.webslingerz.com/jhoffman/congress-email.html

Newsgroups

Many browsers enable users to exchange ideas by using *newsgroups*. A newsgroup is a group of people who participate in a specialized discussion on the Internet. These groups are open forums in which all are welcomed to contribute. Newsgroup postings are sent to a common place for all to read and reply. Some are moderated by an individual or individuals who post items for discussion and moderate any electronic brawls that may ensue. However, not all newsgroups are rife with disagreement. Many offer excellent opportunities for polite conversation with courteous people. All newsgroups provide a place where people can bring new ideas and perspectives to the table. If e-mail is like the postal service, though, newsgroups are like coffee houses on open microphone night.

What is the purpose of the newsgroups if people just contribute ideas and comments on a particular subject? Newsgroups are places where you can ask questions, get ideas, and learn about specific topics. Select a group that has an interest common to yours or a topic that you are trying to learn about. You'll find that there are many newsgroups that focus on humanities, social sciences, and related issues.

The names of newsgroups usually describe their discussion topic. There are several major newsgroup categories. The one you'll use most are the ALT, BIT, and REC groups. REC groups discuss the arts, among others. We've included a list of relevant newsgroups in Appendix II. You'll find some of them interesting and helpful as a supplement to your studies in English Composition and Literature.

> Here is a typical newsgroup URL. Newsgroup names are divided into several descriptive words separated by a period and organized

according to a hierarchy. Note that newsgroup URLs don't use the double slash (//).

news:bit.listserv.literary

Here are the three components:

protocol news:
top category bit
sub category listserv
sub category literary

To configure your browser to connect to a newsgroup, you will need the name of the server computer that handles newsgroups. (Get this from the same people who gave you your mail server address.) You'll perform almost the same procedure you used to set up your e-mail service. To set your newsgroup information, select the *Options* menu and open the *Mail and News Preferences* window. Select the *Servers* tab and you will see the text entry boxes.(Figure 3.10). Once you enter the correct information and restart the browser program, you should be able to view newsgroups. You may find that you can't access some newsgroups. Check to make sure your ISP subscribes to these. If not, they will usually do so if you make a request.

News servers use a protocol called *NetNews Transfer Protocol*, or *NNTP*. You might need to ask around to find out the address for your news server. If you can't find someone to help, you can probably assume that the address for your news server is NEWS.HOST.DOMAIN.

You should now be ready for an adventure. When you use *Naviga-*

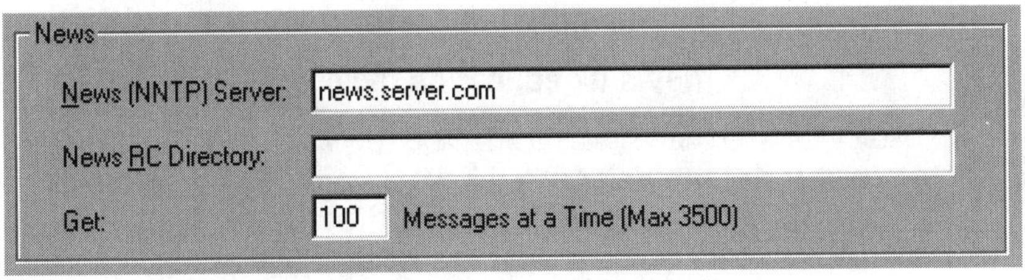

Figure 3.10. With *Navigator*, the dialog window where you will enter the name of your news server can be found in *Mail and News Preferences...* option under the *Options* menu.

tor to read or post articles to newsgroups, you won't be using the same window that you used for browsing the Web. For newsgroups, you'll use what is typically called a *news reader*. To start your news reader, select the Windows option from the menu bar and choose *Netscape News*. A new window will open (Figure 3.11).

Note how this window resembles the Web browser, as well as how it differs. To view a larger list of newsgroups you can select *Options* from the menu bar and choose *Show All Newsgroups*. A larger list of newsgroups will appear on the left. You can subscribe to a specific one by placing a check mark by the desired newsgroup. When you select a newsgroup, the individual articles will appear on the right side of the window. Finally, when you select a specific article, you will see the contents displayed at the bottom of the news reader window. Now, take some time and explore.

The only way to really understand what newsgroups are like is to try them. Here are several newsgroups that will get you started. Connect to one of interest and read some of the postings. For your first time, you should just read the postings and follow some of the conversations. (This is called lurking.) Connections or threads develop between postings as people add comments to earlier postings. As you become familiar with the topic of discussion, you might post a comment yourself. Before you jump in, you may want to read the section titled "Language for the Road" in this chapter.

news:alt.culture.jollyroger

news:bit.listserv.edtech

news:rec.org.sca

news:rec. collectiong.books

news:tnn.literature

news:uk.education.misc

Two useful tools for newsgroups are *DejaNews* and *SIFT*. *DejaNews* (**http://www/dejanews.com/**) allows you to search for topics in newsgroups. *SIFT* (**http://sift.stanford.edu/**) notifies you by e-mail if topics specified by you are discussed. Take a look at both of these!

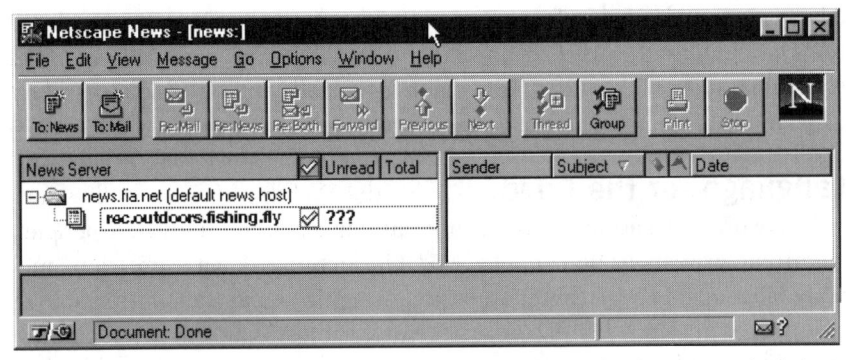

Figure 3.11. *Navigator* includes a built-in news reader. Its features are similar to both the mail client and the Web browser.

Chat

This is yet another avenue for communication. It is probably the one you'll choose if you like to talk. Unlike e-mail and newsgroups, which require you to wait for a response, chat rooms are real-time. This means that you are conversing and observing conversations as they happen. As with newsgroups, it is best to observe the interactions of several chat rooms and read the new user information before you jump in. Some rooms can be excessive and vulgar, but many are frequented by polite people with a genuine desire for conversation. Just like newsgroups, chat rooms are organized by topic and you can usually anticipate the discussion by the name of the group. Unlike newsgroups, there are few academic-specific chat rooms; therefore, you'll probably find that they are a great place for general conversation only.

Just to get you started, here are a few Web-based chat groups. Read the instructions and ask for help if you need it.

WebChat Broadcasting System
http://webchat5.wbs.net/

Jammin's ChatPlanet Chat Room!
http://www.jammin.com/livechat.html

Matt's PaleoChat Room
http://www.pitt.edu/~mattf/PaleoChat.html

Unlike e-mail and newsgroups, you will be frequently asked to login or register before beginning to chat. Often you'll even be given a password.

Always, read the rules for participating and ask for help if you don't understand something. The participants are generally very helpful. The other characteristic of chat rooms is that typically you will use a "handle" or pseudonym when you post a message.

Language for the Road

A few words of caution. Unlike normal conversations between people, electronic exchanges don't convey vocal inflections, facial expression, and body language. (These things aren't easily digitized and transmitted across a copper wire. To be sure, there are such things as Internet telephones and video conferencing, but for most of us they are not affordable and practical.) You will need to practice the way you communicate electronically and be patient when someone misinterprets something you've "said." For example, suppose you tell a joke. Because the reader only gets the text, she may think that you are serious and take offense. Computer people learned about this problem a long time ago and an innovative solution has been developed. The solution is a collection of smileys.

Here are several smileys, but you'll have to tilt your head to the left to interpret them:

:-)   This is a happy face
;-)   This is a wink.
:-(This is a sad face.
:-[This is a really sad face.

Because you eventually will get tired of typing all of the things you want to say, several acronyms are in common use. Here are but a few:

BTW   By The Way
IMHO   In My Humble Opinion
FYI   For Your Information
FAQ   Frequently Asked Question

Now for a couple of terms. Like any other culture, the Internet community has borrowed some common words to describe special situations. Here are two that you'll see:

Flame This refers to the act of yelling, insulting, or degrading a person or his or her character. You can expect to get flamed if you don't follow certain basic rules of *netiquette* (etiquette of the Net).

Spam This refers to the act of posting a comment, message, or advertisement to multiple newsgroups when the note doesn't really pertain to the newsgroup topic. It is the Internet equivalent of sending junk mail.

Here are a few Web resources that you will want to read when you begin communicating online. They are very helpful and entertaining. Enjoy!

E-Mail Etiquette
http://www.iwillfollow.com/email.htm

The Net: User Guidelines and Netiquette By Arlene H. Rinaldi
http://rs6000.adm.fau.edu/rinaldi/net/index.htm

Electronic Frontier Foundation's Unofficial Smiley Dictionary
http://www.eff.org/papers/eegtti/eeg_286.html

Section 3.3
The fun is in the going—Extending

In early Web history, travel was pretty basic. The browser was a piece of software that acted as a totally self-contained vehicle. When you hooked it up, it contained everything you needed to cruise the Net. This has changed. As the Web grows larger, people develop new formats of information they wish to include on the Web. These new formats allow for a richer expression. Things like digital video, audio, animations, interactive games, and 3D worlds are currently very common on the Internet. As people demand more functionality from the Internet, new formats will become available. To cope with this continuing change, Netscape developed a way to add functionality without overloading the basic browser design.

Helpers and Plug-ins

Early Web pages included only text and images. They were much like brochures with the ability to hyperlink to other pages. The images that were included in Web pages were in a GIF format. However, to accommodate new image formats like JPEG, browsers turned to helper applications. If a page designer included a JPEG image, then an external helper application program was used to display the image for viewing outside of the browser. Rather than having to rely on external programs, plug-in programs were developed to add the same features within the browser itself. For example, if you wanted to listen to music across the Internet from your browser, then you could install a plug-in that allows the browser to understand the audio format.

Netscape developed many plug-ins, and they are still the place to turn when you want one. An important thing, though: adding plug-ins to your browser will increase your memory (RAM) requirements. If you add too many plug-ins, your browser might stop working. Only install the plug-ins that you're going to use regularly.

> These addresses will take you to the place where you can download the plug-ins to your computer. These developers also provide a very good description of how to install them and make them work for you.
>
> **RealAudio by Progressive Networks**
>   http://get.real.com/products/player/download.html
>
> **Shockwave by MacroMedia**
>   http://www.macromedia.com/shockwave/download/
>
> **QuickTime by Apple**
>   http://www.quickTime.apple.com/sw/
>
> **Live3D by Netscape**
>   http://home.netscape.com/comprod/products/navigator/live3d/

Once you've lived a little and added a plug-in or two, you can get a list of the ones you've installed right from your browser. Select the *Help* menu and then choose *About Plug-ins*. The browser window will then present a list of all of your installed plug-ins. If you click on the link at the top of the page, you will also be able to connect directly to Netscape's master plug-in page.

Java and JavaScript

Grab a cup of coffee for this one. Helper application programs (helpers) and plug-ins weren't enough to satisfy Web developers. Web developers wanted even more—*more* flexibility, *more* interactivity, and *more* control. *Java* and *JavaScript* were developed to provide *more* that developers wanted. But to understand what *Java* and *JavaScript* are, you need to understand what Web pages *were not*. Web page designers didn't claim to *program* Web pages; rather, they said that they *wrote, designed,* or *created* Web pages. You may wonder what the difference is. Programming is the process of developing a set of instructions that perform a specific function. Writing, designing, and creating are activities that communicate ideas. When executed, programs actively do things, whereas Web pages communicate ideas (by bringing together different media).

One type of media, interactive programs, did not exist in Web pages until the programming languages *Java* and *JavaScript* were made available. Now, besides communicating ideas, Web pages can also interactively do things as well. They add functionality to Web pages just as helpers and plug-ins do, but they provide much greater flexibility. The fundamental difference between the two languages is that *JavaScript* is usually integrated with the Web page and runs on the client side, whereas *Java* is usually integrated on the server side. The results are probably best understood by examining a few *Java* and *JavaScript* programs for yourself. If you are using Netscape *Navigator 2.0* or greater (or Microsoft *Internet Explorer 3.0* or greater), then you have the ability of view and interact with these programs.

The first three URLs will connect you to some really interesting examples of Java.

The Impressionist
http://reality.sgi.com/employees/paul_asd/impression/index.html

Crossword Puzzle
http://home.netscape.com/comprod/products/navigator/version_2.0/java_applets/Crossword

TicTacToe
http://www.javasoft.com:80/applets/TicTacToe/example1.html

This last URL will connect you to a rather large collection of both Java and JavaScript examples.

Gamelan
http://www-b.gamelan.com/index.shtml

Depending on your system, these examples may take a while to load, so please be patient.

Activity
A Talkabout Tour

Learning doesn't stop when you leave the classroom or laboratory. The people around you, textbooks, libraries, and the Internet are all important resources to help you with your education. In particular, the Web, newsgroups, chat rooms, and e-mail can all help you to become well-rounded and well-connected.

E-mail
Because you have a wealth of information at you fingertips, take the time to get some e-mail addresses from the members of your class. Most good e-mail software will provide you with a mechanism to store these addresses for easy retrieval. Begin exchanging e-mail with some of these people and you'll find that there is plenty of help available when you need it.

Newsgroups
Make it a practice to browse newsgroups. Plenty are of general interest; you should also make a habit of checking into a newsgroup that focuses on important topics discussed in class. By visiting many different newsgroups, you'll always have the latest scoop in a variety of subjects.

Chat
Chat rooms may or may not enhance your education. However, you might be able to find a chat room that is relatively empty. If so, arrange a fixed weekly time when you and your classmates can get together to work out problems or discuss material covered that week. A better option is to meet in person, but if this is impossible, chat rooms can provide an alternative.

Web Page
If you are using an ISP for Internet access, then you probably have access to posting information on your homepage. Consider using it as a way to bring other students together for discussion. Check with your instructor and you may find that he or she is willing to help you with this activity.

Chapter 4
Back to the Future
Advanced Techniques

The medium is the message.

No matter how enjoyable and interesting traveling is, it's always good to come home. Traveling in cyberspace is a little bit like traveling through time. It's very easy to lose several hours in what appears to be just a few ticks of the clock. Jet lag is uncomfortable, but virtual time lag may be even more unsettling. All the more reason to have a home in hyperspace to unwind your clock. This chapter will help you design a homepage on the Web and introduce you to setting up a Web server.

To gain the most from this chapter, you will need a few basic skills. You should be capable of creating, moving, and renaming directories and files on your computer. Also, you should be able to install applications onto your computer and set them up to function properly. With these skills, you should be able to follow the concepts outlined in the rest of this chapter. Keep in mind that what follows is not a step-by-step description of Web page design or Web server maintenance, but only an introduction to some basic concepts. You may want to supplement this discussion by consulting additional resources.

Section 4.1
There's no place like home—Designing

The following description will help you create your own homepage. It is not as simple as cruising the Web, but it's not very hard either. Web pages are stored on a Web server. However, you can create a file on your home computer, or even on a floppy disk, that will act as a homepage. Ultimately, you will need access to a Web server to make your homepage part of the Internet. If your campus has a Web server, then they may have a place for student homepages. If you are using an ISP, you will probably be able to post a homepage with them at no additional cost. For the moment, though, let's focus on building a homepage—you don't need to be able to post a homepage in order to understand how to put one together.

Homepages

What good is a homepage? You will find many uses; just a few are mentioned here. A homepage can be used to organize important and frequently accessed links and bookmarks to the Internet, keeping you connected to English Composition and Literature resources all over the world. It's better than a library card.

A homepage can also help you follow personal interests. For example, you can keep links to online magazines, the weather at your favorite camping spots, movie, music, and book reviews, newsgroups, the current news reports, pages with online games, your school's homepage, your friends' pages, the manuals for your e-mail and Web browsers, and your favorite search engines and directories. Some homepages reflect the personality of the owner, who may post information about herself or himself for others to view.

Or imagine designing a homepage and turning it in as homework. You could turn in an assignment with online data, animations, video clips, and sound. You could have graphs that link directly to the data, pictures in color with an audio caption, interactive diagrams to illustrate your point, and an e-mail link if the instructor wanted to ask you a question. Move over word processor!

Now, where is your homepage?!? If you look at Appendix I, you'll see a template for a homepage. It is written in *HTML*, a simple language that Web browsers use to read hypertext documents. The initials stand for *HyperText Markup Language*. Right now, you might want to glance at it just to see what HTML looks like. Later on, you will be able to use this template and customize it as much as you like.

To get an idea of what homepages are like, use the following URLs to see what others have done. Some of these may be appealing to you, others may not—homepage design is a personal choice.

Make A Friend On The Web
   http://albrecht.ecn.purdue.edu/~jbradfor/homepage/
The People Page
   http://www.peoplepage.com/
Laws of Cool Page
   http://humanitas.ucsb.edu/shuttle/cool.html

Just as with cars, you can go manual or automatic when you design a web page. Both methods have advantages and disadvantages. When you design a page manually, you actually write with HTML (like shifting gears for the car). You'll have to learn some rather obscure notations, but you will be able to fully control the look and feel of the page you create. Because most people want an easy way of doing page design, tools have been developed to automate the process. These tools are called *WYSIWYG* (pronounced wizzy-wig) *editors*. (WYSIWYG stands for What You See Is What You Get.) The disadvantage of WYSIWYG tools is that you have less control over page design, but you also save a considerable amount of time. Many designers use WYSIWYG tools for their initial layout and then tweak the HTML code to get what they want. Here is a little bit about each method. It should be enough to get you started.

Automatic

You can use several tools for WYSIWYG design. Some of them let you view the HTML as you design your page; in others, the code is hidden. We will focus on Netscape's WYSIWYG tool, which is called *Navigator Gold*. Basically, it consists of *Navigator* with a built-in editor. (We'll refer to these two parts as the Browser and the Editor.) This software is free to both students and educators and you can get it directly from Netscape across the Internet. Before you read on, download Navigator Gold 3.0 from Netscape's download site and install it on your computer. The address of the site is

http://home.netscape.com/comprod/products/navigator/gold/index.html

---

Choice is a great thing. Instead of relying solely on the information people give you, check for yourself, too. You may turn up something that meets your needs better. Here are a few more WYSIWYG editors for you to evaluate.

Microsoft FrontPage
  http://www.microsoft.com/frontpage/

HoTMetaL Pro
  http://www.sq.com/products/hotmetal/hmp-org.htm

HotDog Pro
  http://www.sausage.com/

> Investigate the numerous WYSIWYG editors on the market carefully. Henry Ford said that when you bought a Model A, you could have any color you wanted as long as it was black. It's the same with some WYSIWYG editors.

Now we're ready to get started. You should have Netscape *Navigator Gold 3.0* installed and an Internet connection. If you select *Options* from the menu bar, you will see an additional preference command titled *Editor Preferences.* . . . Select this and a window will appear (Figure 4.1). Three tabs are found at the top of this preference window. Select the *General* tab and enter your name (as you will soon be an author). You should also enter information for your preferred HTML text editor and image editor.

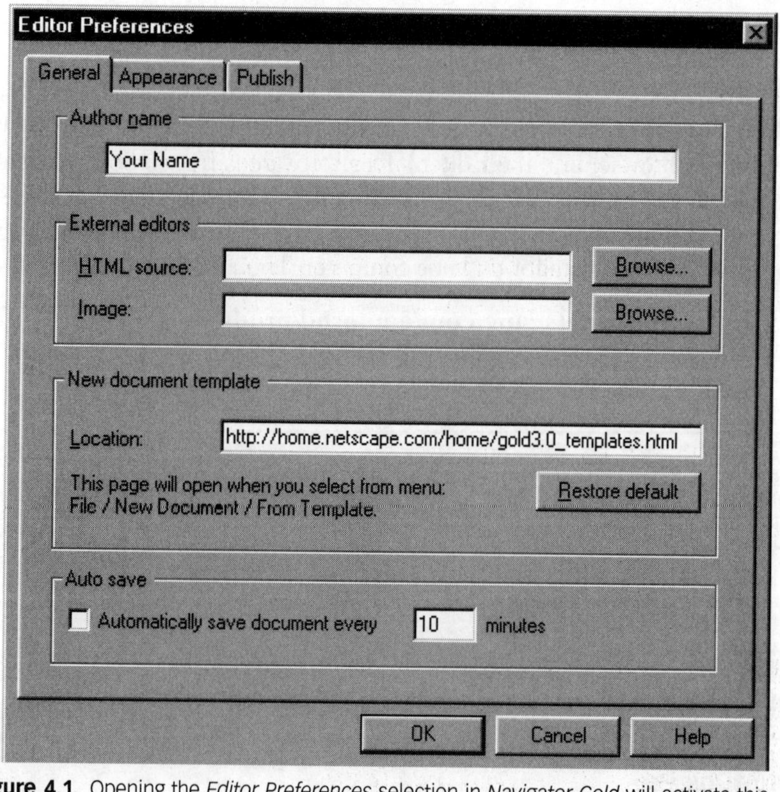

Figure 4.1. Opening the *Editor Preferences* selection in *Navigator Gold* will activate this window.

Are you wondering why you need another HTML editor? Keep in mind that WYSIWYG editors are not the end-all and be-all of document creation. Occasionally you'll want some manual control over both the pages and the images you embed in them. But you don't need to buy any more software. All you need is a simple text editor, which is probably included with your computer. If you are using a Macintosh operating system, you can use either *TeachText* or *SimpleText*. If you are using a Windows-based operating system, you can use either *Notepad* or *Wordpad*. Use the *Browse*. . . button to locate the text editor you'd like to use.

The image editor may not be included with your operating system. However, you don't need one to follow our discussion. When you need one later on, check on the Internet, where numerous image editors are available for free. Use your search engine to locate an image editor.

The next section in the *General* tab is where you enter the URL for a page template source. Don't worry about it now. Select the OK button and your settings will be saved.

Templates

Netscape has organized a wonderful little resource to help first time Web authors. With this, you will quickly and easily write your first page. This is done online and all you need to do is follow along. In no time, you'll have a simple homepage.

To get started, select *File* from the menu bar and choose *New Document* and then choose *From Wizard*. . .(Figure 4.2).You may also use the following URL:

http://home.netscape.com/home/gold3.0_wizard.html

The *Page Wizard* (Figure 4.3) is divided into three unique windows (or frames). Read the basic instructions from the upper right window and select *START* when you are ready.

Once you've started, you'll see a set of instructions in the upper left window. Although the instructions are self-explanatory, a brief

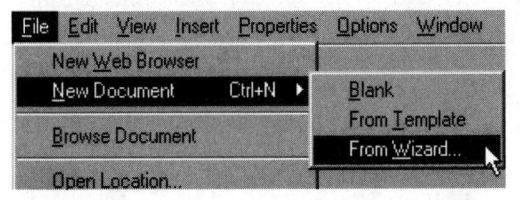

Figure 4.2. Opening *Netscape's Page Wizard* is accessible from the menu bar on *Navigator Gold*.

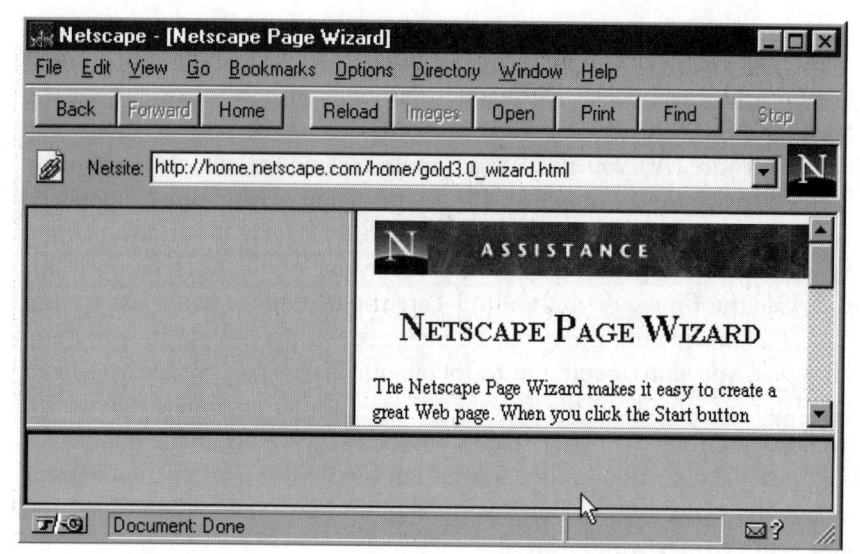

Figure 4.3. *Netscape's Page Wizard* is available only online and you will need to have an Internet connection to use it.

overview of what you need to do is provided here. You'll be essentially working in a counter-clockwise direction.

1. Read the instructions in the left window.
2. Click each hyperlink as you come to it in the instructions.
3. Enter the requested information in the lower window.
4. View the information as it appears in the right window.
5. Modify the information (lower window) until you like what you see.
6. Continue executing the instructions until you get to the end.

When you've executed all of the instructions, select the *Build* button and your first homepage will be displayed in the Browser window.

What have you accomplished so far? Basically, you've used a remote tool (Netscape's *Page Wizard*) to create a homepage from a preset template. Everything that you are now looking at is still on Netscape's server and *not* your computer. You can't do anything more to your homepage until you move it over to your machine.

Select the *Edit* button from the tool bar at the top of the Browser. (If you aren't using the Gold version, you will need to download it from Netscape—it's free.) An Editor window (Figure 4.4) will open along with

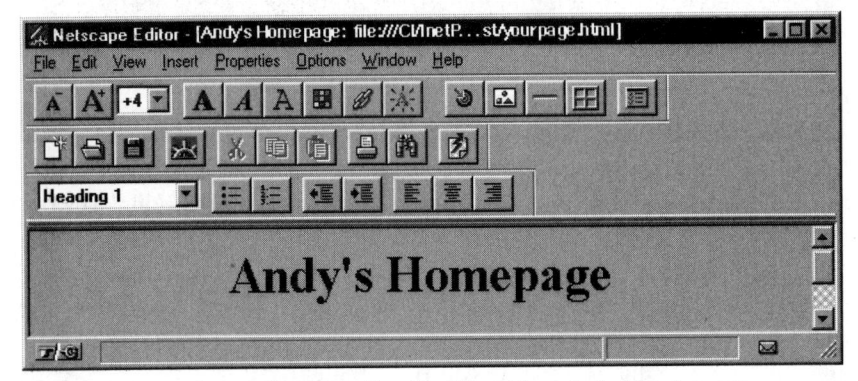

Figure 4.4. The *Editor* window is significantly different from that of the *Browser*

a dialog box asking if you wish to bring over the associated images and preserve the links, which *you do*. You will then get a dialog window in which you can determine the location on your computer where you wish to save the file and images. If you expect to do a lot of Web page design, you should create a directory where you can store all of your pages.

Unlike documents that you may have made with a word processor, Web documents don't combine all of their elements into one package. The text, which consists of words and code, is in a file that has an *.htm* or *.html* suffix. All of the associated elements, which may include images, sounds, and other non-text information, are in separate files with suffixes such as *.gif*, *.jpeg*, and others. *Navigator Gold* brings all of these pieces together when you save a page to your computer.

WYSIWYG

At this point, you still haven't used the Editor portion of *Navigator Gold*. Now that you've saved your new homepage to your local machine, you are ready to add any desired text using the Editor.

Let's review the work you've completed so far. With Netscape *Navigator Gold* installed, you used the *Page Wizard* and generated a simple homepage from a template. You downloaded that page to your server and then you opened it in the Editor portion of *Navigator Gold*. There are also other templates available at the Netscape site. You can save them or any other page in this same way. (Note, however, that some pages you'll find on the Web contain copyrighted information.)

Next, let's do a couple of things so you can see how easy it is to use the Editor. Then you can experiment with the software to explore all your options. Later on you might want to check out your local bookstore to learn more about designing Web pages. You'll find a great selection of books that will help you to understand all of the details of *Navigator Gold* or any other WYSIWYG editor.

To familiarize yourself with the Editor, move your cursor over the top of each Editor button and pause (but don't click the mouse button) until the label appears. Reading the labels should help you discover the function of each button.

Remember to always save your original page! This means that after you've done something cool to your page, save it as a different file. By doing so, you can always retrieve the last page if you realize that your change wasn't really as great as you first thought.

Here are a couple of things to do to your homepage that will start you on your way.

1. Modify (size, color, style, etc.) the text on your page.
2. Enter a new paragraph of text.
3. Enter a bulleted list of information.
4. Place a horizontal line.
5. Insert an image.
6. Embed a link to an email address.
7. Embed a link to an URL on the Web.
8. Create a new document and then embed a link from your homepage to this new document.

Here are two great sites to help you learn more about designing a Web page. You'll find images, icons, backgrounds, and a lot of guidance.

Netscape Gold Authoring Guide
http://home.netscape.com/eng/mozilla/3.0/handbook/authoring/navgold.htm

Netscape's Gold Rush Tool Chest
http://home.netscape.com/assist/net_sites/starter/samples/index.html

Hint: To capture an image you need only to be able to see it. For Macintosh users, click on the image and just hold down a second longer than you normally would. A window will appear with save options. For *Windows*, use the right mouse button and you'll get the same options window.

Now you have a homepage! Right? Well, don't worry if it still isn't perfect. You have plenty of time to make it shine. Or you may be perfectly satisfied with what you created using the Editor. If so, you may want to read the next section at a later date. In it, we will explain a little bit about how to take the manual design approach by using HTML. The extra effort may be well worthwhile if you plan to create Web sites that are more complex.

Take a look at the HTML code of the page you just created. While you have the Editor window active, select View from the menu bar and then select Edit Document Source (Figure 4.5). This will open the text editor you designated in the Editor Preferences and display the HTML code for your page.

You may want to print a copy of the HTML code in your homepage. Unless you got carried away with the Editor, this will allow you to see your homepage on one or two sheets.

Manual

The HTML code on your homepage is really pretty easy to understand. You need to remember only a couple of things in order to read HTML. For the moment, ignore the HTML and focus on the rest of the document—you'll see that it makes sense. You can do this by alternately viewing your homepage file through Navigator and then through your text editor. You don't need a fancy program to write or edit HTML, just a text editor and an understanding of the code.

Now, look at the window with the HTML code. At the very top you'll see a tag like this: <HTML>. A tag is an element of HTML code. It is added to the page to emphasize the text that will appear on the viewed Web page. Tags always have an angle bracket (<) followed by one or more letters and a reverse angle bracket (>). Here are some examples: <BODY>, <HEAD>, and <TITLE>.

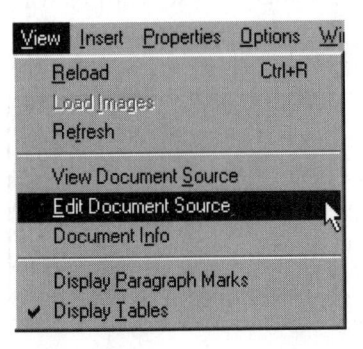

Figure 4.5. This pull-down menu is available only while the Editor portion of *Navigator Gold* is active. *View Document Source* will display the source but will not allow you to modify it. *Edit Document Source* will allow you to modify the HTML code.

Most HTML tags come in pairs. For example, the tag <HEAD>, found on the second line of the program, is accompanied by a corresponding tag </HEAD> (see the fourth line). The second member of each tag pair has a forward slash (/) preceding the word. Here are the other members of tag pairs: </BODY>, and </TITLE>. Tags, when used in sets or pairs, surround a section of text and define the beginning and end of an HTML section. It is possible to use tags incorrectly just as it is possible to use English incorrectly. Here is an example of a properly coded HTML page:

<HTML>
<HEAD>
This is where a description and purpose of the page is written. The material is not viewed on the browser. It is only used to document the intent of the page.
</HEAD>
<BODY>
This is where the material that is to be viewed through the browser will be written.
</BODY>
</HTML>

All properly coded HTML documents have this basic format. Notice the beginning and ending member of each tag pair. Although tags usually operate in pairs, some are used as solitary tags. When you want to separate sections of text with two spaces, you could use the paragraph tag, <P>. Two line break tags, <BR>, will also do the same thing. If you want the browser to make a horizontal line across the viewed page, then you use a horizontal line tag, <HR>. You may have noticed that the tag names are abbreviations of what they do. You don't have to learn everything about HTML now, however. You can embed some of these features with your WYSIWYG editor.

If you really want to jump into HTML, here are a few Web sites that may be a helpful to you.

Netscape Page Starter Site
http://home.netscape.com/home/starter.html

> **Webreference**
> http://ww.webreference.com/
>
> **Web Page Construction**
> http://saturn.med.nyu.edu/~wei/webpage.html

Other people have already written cool homepages and you might want to use theirs as a template if you don't like yours or the one in Appendix I. Simply find the interesting pages that other people have developed. Copy the code and modify it to reflect your personality.

Hyperlinks

One very important element in HTML is the code for hyperlinks (jumping points within Web pages). You know most of what you need to know to create hyperlinks. The HTML tag pair for a hyperlink is <A> and </A>. There are two main components to a link. The first element is the URL of the document to which the link leads, and the second is the word (or words) to be set as a hyperlink. You can also enter links into your pages with the Editor. Here is an example of how to write a link tag.

    <A HREF="URL">
       Word
    </A>

This may seem a little complicated, but it's not that hard. The first line of the example above begins the code for a link. The letters and signs between the angle brackets represent an URL, which tells the browser the location of the requested document. The second line is the hypertext link that will appear in color on the Web page. The link tag pair is completed with the ending link tag, </A>. When on an actual Web page, the hypertext link can be selected by a user, who will be sent to the page specified by the URL.

> In this exercise, use your text editor and type in the basic page elements discussed earlier (<HTML> and </HTML>). Within the body of the page, type in a link tag pair using a real URL. Use one or all of the

examples provided below. Once you have this page, save it with the name TEST.HTML and view it with your browser. (You do not have to be online for any of this.)

A Beginners Guide to HTML
http://www.ncsa.uiuc.edu/General/Internet/WWW/HTMLPrimer.html

How to Publish on the Web
http://www.thegiim.org/

The Bare Bones Guide to HTML
http://werbach.com/barebones/

See step 2 in the section below for help in finding and displaying the file. Once you've got this page up and running on your browser, try the hyperlink online. Does it work? These URLs should take you to resources that will tell you more about Web publishing.

Home

You now have a homepage. Where do you put it to make it work? This depends on whether you will have access to a Web server or not. The instructions that follow assume that you don't have access. Once you've completed your homepage, you'll have a file on either your hard drive or a floppy disk. The advantage of having your homepage on floppy disk is that you'll have a portable homepage that you can use on any computer. Here is a five-step procedure for finding and setting your default homepage to the one you've created.

1. After you finished the end-of-chapter activity, you should copy your intended homepage to either a floppy disk or your hard drive.
2. With *Navigator*, you should be able to find a command under the *File* menu called *Open File...* If you initiate this command, you'll get a dialog window where you can designate the file you wish to open. You want to open your homepage which at the moment is not on a server. Select the HTML file for your homepage from either your floppy disk or hard drive and press the *Return* key. Your browser will open your homepage and display it for you.

3. If it isn't set already, change your *Options* setting so you can view the URLs of the pages that are displayed on your browser. When this is set properly, you'll notice that your file's URL is listed something like this: file:///............/file.html. The protocol is no longer HTTP and there are more than two slashes.
4. Record this URL on a piece of paper so that you can refer to it in the next step. (Every slash and colon is significant.)
5. Earlier in this chapter, we discussed how to change the homepage designation for your browser. First, open the *General Preferences* section of the *Options* menu. Then select the *General* tab and enter the URL that you wrote down in step 4 into the homepage entry window.

Now that you've performed these steps, your browser should automatically jump to your homepage when you select the *Home* button from the toolbar. Give it a try. The procedures that you've just performed have allowed your browser to memorize the location of your homepage file. If you move it or erase it, you'll have to do this *all* over again.

The Future

If you want to learn more about tags, it's not hard to do so. Various places on the Web offer online tutorials on HTML design. Links to some of these places are found in the homepage template provided in Appendix I. As you learn more about the Internet and HTML, you'll discover ways to manually add pictures to your pages. Later you'll even begin adding sounds and maybe a video clip or two. The tools available to you today barely hint at what will be available to you in the future.

Section 4.2
Opening your own shop—Serving

A few of you may want to assemble and maintain an active Web server. If so, you'll need an extra measure of determination. A Web server is not necessarily easy to manage; you'll need to develop skills beyond those required to cruise the Net. However, doing so is well within your ability if you know how to get help and find resources. This enterprise will require a considerable amount of time, equipment, and money. But it will give you more control.

The Shopping List

To set up a server on the Web, you need four basic components:

- Computer
- Software
- Internet Connection
- A Willing Participant

It's the last element of the list that stops most people. If you are going to set up a server, then you need someone who is willing *and* able to spend a considerable amount of time maintaining and managing it. If this someone is you, make sure you have the time and energy for it.

Because of the many tasks it must perform, the computer server should be dedicated to that purpose alone. The following list contains suggestions for a basic server.

Hardware:
- Pentium computer (100 MHz)
- 36 MB RAM
- 1 GB Hard Drive
- CD-ROM Drive
- Network Interface Card
- Keyboard and Monitor

Software:
- Server Operating System
- Web Server Software
- Mail and News Server Software (Optional)

Connection:
- ISDN or T1

We suggest a *Pentium* because they are relatively cheap and common. You don't need a really fast system like a *Pentium Pro* because a server typically doesn't need speed, just the bandwidth for the Internet connection. A *Pentium* also offers the flexibility of serving files to both *Macintosh* computers and PCs.

System memory is important if you want to run multiple elements like a mail server and a news server. The same goes for the hard drive. You'll need some storage, but keep in mind that you can always add to your system later on: Hard drives continue to get cheaper, faster, and larger. If you don't need extra memory and storage now, then wait and save your money. The CD-ROM is probably essential if you have to do any software installation. Without it, you'll quickly learn how time consuming it can be to install software for one program using, say, 50 floppy disks. The network interface card is used to connect your computer to your network (campus or outside provider). Take your provider's suggestions when purchasing the network card. The monitor (and keyboard) need not be expensive because you won't be doing any fancy graphic work.

For the software we suggest *Windows NT 4.0 Server* as the base operating system: It is cheap, powerful, easy to use, growing in popularity (this means you'll be able to get lots of help), and can handle a mix of both *Macintosh* computers and PCs. A great deal of software is currently being developed for *Windows NT*, so you won't have a difficult time finding compatible application programs.

For Web server software, Microsoft *Internet Information Server (IIS)* is included free with the *Windows NT*. Netscape also provides Web server software for *Windows NT*. It, too, is free. The *IIS* software may be slightly more intuitive to use, but you may find otherwise. Try them both. If you're interested in setting up a mail or news server, you will need additional software. These come in separate packages and are also commonly available from both Microsoft and Netscape. Our advice is to start with a Web server and add more when you're comfortable with what you've created.

The components of a Web server are not unduly expensive—the computer and software will probably cost you less than $5000 in today's market. However, hardware and software are not your only expenses. A Web server without a network connection is nearly useless. Even if you want to set up an internal network (Intranet), you'll need the basic wires and connections to other computers. Keep in mind that your school may be able to make a Web server possible by providing computer resources that would otherwise be too expensive to purchase. If your school cannot offer such assistance, you will have to rent Internet access on a monthly basis. This will probably cost a considerable amount of money. Thus, be sure that you have a compelling need for a server before you begin to assemble one.

If you do put together a server, you may need additional equipment to ensure its security, such as a tape backup system and an uninterruptible power supply (UPS). If your information is really valuable, you may want to even consider locking everything in a back room with a redundant server.

If you're determined to build a Web server, the following Web sites describe how to set up, maintain, and administer a Windows NT server. You'll also be able to download free versions of Web server software from Microsoft, Netscape, and other companies.

Web66 Windows NT Cookbook
http://web66.coled.umn.edu/WinNT/CookBook/Default.html

Windows NT Utilities
http://www.ime.net/~peteb/

Netscape's Education Program
http://home.netscape.com/comprod/server_central/edu_drive.html

Microsoft's Education Program
http://www.microsoft.com/education/hed/default.htm

Activity
Show that You've Arrived

If you've been reading this chapter with your hands on a computer keyboard, then you're close to having a homepage of your own. This final activity is designed to take you the rest of the way. Using the template provided in Appendix I, you will be able to build a homepage that you can keep on a floppy disk.

We use several different fonts in order to distinguish various elements of the homepage template in Appendix I. *Large italic font* is used to represent the text that you are to replace with your information. HTML tags are represented in a <SMALLER FONT, ALL IN UPPER-CASE AND WITH ANGLE BRACKETS>. Text that is not an HTML tag and *does not* need to be changed is in a regular size and font.

If you would like to consider several alternatives, you can find other homepage templates at **http://www-pcd.stanford.edu/mognes/intro/templates.html**. But take the time now to add some flash to whatever template you choose. After you have completed entering your information, save your work (either to a floppy or hard disk) using a file name, say HOMENAME, with an HTML suffix (that is, save the file as HOMENAME.HTML). You can use the file on your home computer, or you can post it on your campus Web server or your ISP.

If you choose to post your homepage on your campus Web server or with your ISP, register your site at **http://www.liquidimaging.com/liqimg/submit/submit.html** to make sure your homepage is listed in the Web directories and search engines. With world-wide exposure, you will have indeed arrived. See you on the Web!

Appendix I
Stepping Out
Student Homepage Template

In the electric age we wear all mankind as our skin.

```
<HTML>
<HEAD>
       <TITLE>Your Homepage</TITLE>
</HEAD>

<BODY>
<CENTER>
       <H1>Your Name</H1>
       <H2>Your Title, Major, or Philosophy of Life</H2>
       <H3>
       <ADDRESS>
              Your address<BR>
              May<BR>
              Go<BR>
              Here<BR>
              <P>
              Your e-mail address<BR>
       </ADDRESS>
       </H3>
</CENTER>
<HR>

<DL>
       <H2>This Is Your Life:</H2>
       <DD>Just say something about yourself. After you've added some
              information to your homepage file, compare it to what actually
```

shows on your browser. You'll notice that most of the HTML code is not visible.
<P>
<DD>*You can have as many paragraphs as you wish. Here's another paragraph.*
<P>
</DL>
<DL>

<H2>*Important Resources*</H2>
<DD>
<A HREF="http://www.ssnewslink.com">
NewsLink from Simon and Schuster
</A>
</DL>
<HR>
<DL>

<H2>Handbooks and Manuals</H2>
<DD>
<A HREF="http://www.matisse.net/files/glossary.html">
Glossary of Internet Terms
</A>
<DD>
<A HREF="http://home.netscape.com/eng/mozilla/3.0/handbook/">
Netscape Handbook
</A>
<DD>
<A HREF="http://home.netscape.com/eng/mozilla/3.0/handbook/authoring/navgold.htm">
Netscape Gold Authoring Guide
</A>
</DL>
<HR>
<DL>

<H2>Directories and Search Engines: </H2>
<DD>
<A HREF="http://www.lycos.com">
Lycos Search Engine
</A>

```
        <DD>
                <A HREF="http://www.webcrawler.com/">
                        WebCrawler Search Engine
                </A>
        <DD>
                <A HREF="http://www.yahoo.com/">
                        Yahoo Directory
                </A>
</DL>
<HR>
<DL>
        <H2>Design and Publish: </H2>
        <DD>
                <A HREF="http://www.ncsa.uiuc.edu/General/Internet/WWW/HTMLPrimer.html">
                        A Beginner's Guide to HTML
                </A>
        <DD>
                <A HREF="http://werbach.com/barebones/">
                        The BareBones Guide to HTML
                </A>
        <DD>
                <A HREF="http://www.thegiim.org/">
                        How to Publish On The Web
                </A>
        <DD>
                <A HREF="http://home.netscape.com/assist/net_sites/starter/samples/index.html">
                        Netscape's Gold Rush Tool Chest
                </A>
</DL>
<HR>
<DL>
        <H2>English Composition and Literature Tools: </H2>
        <DD>
                <A HREF="http://www.oed.coml">
                        Oxford English Dictionary
                </A>
```

```
        <DD>
                <A HREF="http://www.akweb.com/singles/websters.htm">
                    Webster's Dictionary
                </A>
<DD>
                <A HREF="http://www.columbia.edu/acis/bartelby/strunk">
                    Strunk and White's Elements of Style
                </A>
<DD>
                <A HREF="http://owl.english.purdue.edu/">
                    Purdue University On Line Writing Lab
                </A>
<DD>
                <A HREF="http://humanitas.ucsb.edu/shuttle/techwrit.html">
                    Hypertext and Electronic Media
                </A>
<DD>
                <A HREF="http://www.ind.net/Internet/comp.html">
                    World Wide Web Sources for Rhetoric and Composition
                </A>
<DD>
                <A HREF="http://humanitas.ucsb.edu/shuttle/english.html">
                    Voice of the Shuttle
                </A>
</DL>
<HR>
<H3>
        Your Name <A HREF="mailto:Name@server.edu">e-mail address<\A>
</H3>

</BODY>
</HTML>
```

Appendix II
Sock it to me
Internet Resources for English Composition and Literature

A hot medium is one that extends the single sense in "high definition." High definition is the state of being filled with data.

Here are a number of links that you should find "ve-e-ry interesting." Think of this as a starter kit for further investigation. We include Web sites for Using the Internet, Digital Library Web sites, and General Web sites for English Composition and Literature.

We have one final suggestion. Prentice Hall now provides active Web sites for many of the textbooks it publishes. (You are likely using one with this manual.) To access these sites simply type in the individual Web site URLs listed below. These sites contain numerous links to English resources on the Internet. Simply go to the sites indicated and select the sections entitled "Web Links" or "Destinations." These Prentice Hall Web sites have the added advantage of providing active links to many of the resources you will find below. Thus, you can avoid some of the problems encountered from having to type out long, frequently complicated URL addresses. The Prentice Hall English URLs are:

Fulwiler/Hayakawa THE BLAIR HANDBOOK Second Edition
http://www.prenhall.com/fulwiler

Hawisher LITERACY, TECHNOLOGY, AND SOCIETY
http://www.prenhall.com/hawisher

Miller NEW WAYS OF WRITING
http://www.prenhall.com/miller

Rodrigues RESEARCH PAPER AND THE WORLD WIDE WEB
http://www.prenhall.com/rodrigues

Several comments are in order before you begin surfing. First, don't be discouraged if your first try to link to a site produces a message like "Unable to connect to remote host." The rule of thumb is to try the same site three times in a row before proceeding to another URL. (Remember, you're still trying to communicate with the World Wide Wait.) Second, be careful typing site locations. If you mistype one character (capital letters matter), the address won't work. Third, Web sites come and go more often than print media. What is on the Internet today may be gone tomorrow. Fourth, a tilde (~) usually designates a site maintained by a person, rather than an organization or some "non-person." These are the sites most likely to disappear on the Web. Finally, we list just a few newsgroups. If you are an archaeologist (or anyone who has done some digging), there are more newsgroups than you could possibly dream of excavating. Try **http://www.tile.net/tile/news/** to unearth your favorite newsgroup. Get down!

Websites for Using the Internet

Internet Starter Kit (Simon and Schuster Publishers)
http://www.mcp.com/hayden/iskm/book.html

Resources for Web Surfers
http://www.w3.org/pub/WWW/

World Wide Web FAQ
http://sunsite.unc.edu/boutell/faq/

Learn the Net
http://www.paradesa.com/teionline/home/home.html

Understanding and Using the Internet
http://www2.pbs.org/uti/

Newbie Training
http://www.newbie.net/CyberCourse

Interactive Guide to the Internet
http://www.sierramm.com/smpnet.html

Search Engines

Webcrawler
http://www.webcrawler.com

Yahoo
http://www.yahoo.com

Alta Vista
http://altacista.digital.com

Lycos
http://www.irsociety.com:80/wbs/lycos.html

Excite
http://www.excite.com/query.html

Infoseek
http://www.infoseek.com/

Hotbot
http://www.hotbot.com/

Research Tools

Oxford English Dictionary
http:www.oed.com

Roget's Thesaurus
http://humanities.uchicago.edu/forms_unrest/ROGET.html

Bartlett's Familiar Quotations
http://www.columbia.edu/acis/bartleby/barlett

Webster's Dictionary
http://www.akweb.com/singles/websters.htm
http://www.digicity.com/eng_0075.htm

CARLUnCover
http://www.carl.org/uncover/

MLA-Style Citations of Electronic Sources
http://www.cas.usf.edu/english/walker/mla.html

APA-Style Citations of Electronic Sources
http://www.cas.usf.edu/english/walker/apa.html

Digital Library Websites

Stanford University
http://diglib.stanford.edu/

University of California at Berkeley
http://elib.cs.berkeley.edu/

University of Michigan
http://http2.sils.umich.edu/UMDL/HomePage.html

University of Illinois
http://www.grainger.uiuc.edu/dli/

University of California at Santa Barbara
http://alexandria.sdc.ucsb.edu/

Carnegie Mellon University
http://fuzine.mt.cs.cmu.edu/im/

Library of Congress Digital Library
http://www.loc.gov/

Berkeley Digital Library SunSITE
http://sunsite.berkeley.edu/

Digitral Libraries Research
http://www.nlc-bnc.ca/cgi-bin/iflalwgate/DIGLIB/

Humanities Texts
http://english-server.hss.cmu.edu

eLib Homepage
http://ukoln.bath.ac.uk/elib/

The Electric Library
http://www.elibrary.com/

Project Gutenberg - Great Works of Literature
http://jg.cso.uiuc.edu/PG/welcome.html

Writing

Strunk and White's Elements of Style
http://www.columbia.edu/acis/bartleby/strunk/

Copyright Web Page
http://www.benedict.com

Inkspot: A Resource for Writers
http://www.inkspot.com/~ohi/inkspot/

Rhyming Dictionary
http://www.cs.cmu.edu/~dougb/rhyme.html

Classics

The Library of Congress Resources for Greek and Latin Classics
http://lcweb.loc.gov/global/classics/classics.html

Greek Mythology
http://www.intergate.net/uhtml/.jhunt/greek_myth/greek_myth.html

Virtual Tour of the Acropolis
http://www.mechan.ntua.gr/webacropol/

Diotima: Women and Gender in the Ancient World
http://www.uky.edu/ArtsSciences/Classics/gender.html

Perseus Project
http://medusa.perseus.tufts.edu

Old English

Beowulf
http://www.uky.edu/ArtsSciences/English/Beowulf

Geoffrey Chaucer
http://www.alchemyweb.com/%7Ealchemy/englit/medlit/chaucer.htm

Sir Gawain and the Green Knight
http://www.netreach.net:80/~alchemy/englit/medlit/gawain.htm

The Labyrinth
http://www.georgetown.edu/labyrinth/labyrinth-home.html

WWW Medieval Resources
http://ebbs.english.vt.edu/medieval.ebbs.html

Renaissance and 17th Century

Center for Reformation and Renaissance Studies
http://citd.scar.utoronto.ca/renaissance/renaissance.html

Milton
http://www.urich.edu/~creamer/milton.html

Dante
http://www.nd.edu/~italnet/Dante

William Shakespeare
http://www.shakespeare.com

Edmund Spenser
http://darkeing.uoregon.edu/~rbear

John Donne
http://uslink.net/~snoopy/donne.html

Voice of the Shuttle -Renaissance and 17th Century Sites
http://humanitas/ucsb/edu/shuttle/eng-ren.html#general

18th Century

Voice of the Shuttle -18th Century Sites
http://humanitas/ucsb/edu/shuttle/eng-ren.html#general

18th Century pages by Jack Lynch
http://www.english.upenn.edu/~jlynch/18th

Alexander Pope
http://www-unix.oit.umass.edu/~sconstan/

Samuel Johnson
http://dept.english.upenn.edu/~jlynch/Johnson/

Aphra Behn
http://ernie.bgsu.edu/~smorgan/publick/behn.html

William Congreve
http://ernie.bgsu.edu/~smorgan/publick/congreve.html

Joanathan Swift
http://www.mala.bc.ca/~mcneil/swift.htm

John Dryden
http://library.utoronto.ca//www/utel/rp/authors/dryden.html

Nineteenth Century British

Voice of the Shuttle - Romantics
http://humanitas/ucsb/edu/shuttle/eng-rom.html

Voice of the Shuttle - Victorian
http://humanitas/ucsb/edu/shuttle/eng-vic.html

Jane Austen
http://uts.cc.utexas.edu/~churchh/janeinfo.html#janetoc

William Blake
http://world.std.com/%7Ealbright/blake.html
http://www.aa.net/%7Eurizen/blake2.html

Samuel Coleridge
http://www.lib.virginia.edu/etext/stc/Coleridge/

Lewis Carroll
http://www.students.uiuc.edu/~jbirenba/carroll.html

Alfred Tennyson
http://charon.sfsu.edu/tennyson/tennyson.html

Mary Wollstonecraft
http://www.ehche.ac.uk:80/college/schools/human/english/mw.htm

William Wordsworth
http://www.cc.columbia.edu/acis/bartleby/wordsworth/index.html

John Keats
http://www.columbia.edu/acis/bartleby.keats/index.html

Thomas Paine
http://grid.let.rug.nl/~welling/usa/paine.html

Literature: Victorian Era
http://www.jmu.edu:80/libliaison/ebbscm/vict.htm

George Eliot
http://www.bogo.co.uk/emlyn/GEORGEELIOT.HTML

Elizabeth Barrett Browning
http://mirrors.org.sg:80/victorian/ebb/ebbioov.html

The Victorian Web
http://www.stg.brown.edu:80/projects/hypertext/landow/victorian/vn/vicauth2.html

Twentieth Century British and Irish

Voice of the Shuttle -Modern British
http://humanitas/ucsb/edu/shuttle/eng-mod.html#british

Voice of the Shuttle - British
http://humanitas/ucsb/edu/shuttle/eng-cont.html#british

Sherlockian Page
http://watserv1.uwaterloo.ca/%7Ecredmond/sh.html

TS Eliot
http://www-scf.usc.edu:80/~alozano/eliot.html

W B Yeats
http://www.lit.kobe-u.ac.jp/~hishika/yeats.htm

James Joyce in Cyberspace
http://astro.ocis.temple.edu/~callahan/joyce.html/

Joseph Conrad
http://www.mala.bc.ca:80/~mcneil/conrad.htm

Virginia Woolf
http://www.clark.net/pub/cosmic/woolf7.html

Samuel Beckett
http://www-personal.umich.edu:80/~kadaca/bnormal.html

George Bernard Shaw
http://www.zia.com:80/arts/literature/englit/shaw/#top

Early American

Voice of the Shuttle
http://humanitas/ucsb/edu/shuttle/eng-amer.html#colonial

Benjamin Franklin
http://grid.let.rug.nl/~welling/usa/franklin.html
http://nisc8.upenn.edu/AR/men/bf.html

Thomas Paine
http://www.dpipc.com/cdadesign/paine/home.html

Nineteenth Century American

19th Century American Women Writers Web
http://clever.net/19cwww/

Ralph Waldo Emerson
http://www.calpoly.edu:80/~jhardest/emerson.html

Stephen Crane
http://www.en.utexas.edu/~mmaynard/Crane/crane.html

Emily Dickinson
http://lal.cs.byu.edu/people/black/dickinson.html

Herman Melville
http://www.melville.org

Edgar Allan Poe
http://www.zia.com/arts/literature/uslit/poe/

Walt Whitman
http://www.vive.com:80/connect/walt/whit.htm

Mark Twain
http://web.syr.edu/~fjzwick/twainwww.html

Henry David Thoreau
http://www.ecotopia.org:80/ehof/thoreau/links.html

Twentieth Century American

Voice of the Shuttle
http://humanitas/ucsb/edu/shuttle/eng-cont.html#american

The Beat's Page
http://www.charm.net/~brooklyn/LitKicks.html

The Elizabeth Bishop Site
http://www.en.utexas.edu/~daniel/bishop

Ralph Ellison
http://www.levity.com/corduroy/ellison.htm

William Faulkner
http://www.mcsr.olemiss.edu/~egjbp/faulkner/index.html

F. Scott Fitzgerald
http://www.sc.edu/fitzgerald/index.html

Ernest Hemingway
http://rio.atlantic.net:80/~gagne/hem/hem.html

Arthur Miller
http://www.levity.com:80/corduroy/millera.htm

Walker Percy
http://sunsite.unc.edu/wpercy/

J. D. Salinger
http://www.levity.com/corduroy/salinger.htm

Wallace Stevens
http://www.wesleyan.edu:80/wstevens/stevens.html

Thorton Wilder
http://www.levity.com/corduroy/wilder.htm

Sylvia Plath
http://www.informatik.uni-leipzig.de/privat2/beckmann/public_html/plath.html

Robert Frost
http://144.96.211.125/frost/index.html

Alice Walker
http://www.alchemyweb.com/~alchemy/alicew/

Rhetoric and Composition

Hypertext and Electronic Media
http://humanitas.ucsb.edu/shuttle/techwrit.html

World Wide Web Sources for Rhetoric and Composition
http://www.ind.net/Internet/comp.html

The Blue Ribbon Campaign
http://www.eff.org/blueribbon.html

RhetNet
http://www.missouri.edu/~rhetnet/

English and Composition Classes
http://www.utexas.edu/world/lecture/e/
http://www.csubak.edu/~ethiroux/305/305top.htmlx

English Department Home Pages
http://ernie.lang.nagoya-u.ac.jp/~matsuoka/Dept-Eng.html#USA
http://www.csubak.edu/home/acadpro/departments/english/

Cooperative/Collaborative Learning

MOO (Multiple Object Oriented)
Moo's are real time discussion groups on a variety of topics. They can be accessed using Telnet which should be available through your institution. For more information on how they operate, go to
http://www.itp.berkeley.edu/~thorne/MOO.html

Brown Hypertext Hotel
telnet 128.148.37.8 8888 or
telnet duke.cs.brown.edu 1709

College Town
telnet patty.bvu.edu 7777

Daedalus Moo
telnet daedalus.com 777

Diversity University
telnet moo.du.org 8888

Virtual Online University
telnet brazos.iac.net.8888

Write MUX
telnet writemux.visi.com 6250

Online Writing Labs: OWL's

Online writing labs provide services from handouts on grammar and punctuation to actual reviewing of your writing. They vary considerably in form and content.

University of Maine
http://www.ume.maine.edu/~wcenter/others.html

Bowling Green State University
http://www.bgsu.edu/departments/writing-lab/Homepage.html

Carnegie-Mellon
http://english-server.hss.cmu.edu/

Dakota State University
http://www.dsu.edu/departments/liberal/owl/

Michigan Technological University
http://www.hu.mtu.edu/~jdcolman/wc/welcome.html

Purdue
http://owl.english.purdue.edu/

Temple University
gopher://astro.ocis.temple.edu/11/Writing%20Center

Trinity College
http://www.trincoll.edu/writcent/aksmith.html

Virginia Tech
http://athena.english.vt.edu/owl_www/owl.html

University of Arkansas
gopher://rscc.cc.tn.us/11gopher_root%3a%5bdata.wcs%5d

University of Michigan
http://www.umich.edu/~nesta/OWL/owl.html

University of Missouri
http://www.missouri.edu/~wleric/writery.html

University of Oregon
http://darkwing.uoregon.edu/~jcross/word.html

University of Toledo
gopher://gopher.utoledo.edu/11GOPHER_ROOT%3A%5B_
CAMPUS-INFO.DEPARTMENTS-AND-DIVISIONS.
uts-writing-center%5D

Online Writing Laboratory
http://athena.english.vt.edu/OWL_WWW/owl.html

General Websites for Humanities and Social Sciences

The HUMBUL Gateway: International Resources for the Humanities
http://info.ox.ac.uk/departments/humanities/international.html

The WWW Virtual Library
http://www.w3.org/hypertext/DataSources/bySubject/
Overview.html

Voice of the Shuttle Guide to the Humanities and Social Sciences
http://humanities.ucsb.edu/

Research Resources for Graduate Students
http://www.tgsa.com/altpages/rbutters.html

Forum on Technology, Media and Society
http://www.arts.acsb.edu:80/~speed/

English Composition/Literature Newsgroups

These newsgroups can be accessed using the News reader of Netscape.

alt.books.reviews
alt.culture.jollyroger

alt.education
alt.education.email-project
alt.education.research
alt.gothic
alt.journalism
alt.support.learning-disab
bit.listserv.wac1
bit.listserv.edtech
bit.listserv.literary
bit.listserv.tesl.1
humanities.lit.author
misc.writing
misc.writing.screenplays
rec.arts.books
rec.arts.books.children
rec.collecting.books
rec.org.sca
relcom.education
sco.college.gradinfo
tnn.literature
uk.education.misc

Appendix III
Documenting Your Electronic Sources

Living in an era dubbed "The Age of Information," knowledge and words are taking on more significance than ever. When people started realizing that income could be made by selling their words, copyright laws came into effect. While evolving, those laws are still in effect requiring writers to give credit to the source for information they use in their own writing. For the sake of uniformity, style manuals were developed by different organizations dictating how the documentation should be done. When writing in English Composition and Literature, the Modern Language Association (MLA) and the American Psychological Association (APA) are the most commonly used style guidelines, but others are available, such as *The Chicago Manual of Style* (CMS). Always find out from your instructor the style you will be expected to use for your writing assignment so that you can follow the appropriate guidelines. Because the available methods of obtaining electronic information are developing so rapidly, the printed style manuals have had difficulty keeping up with the changes. If you do a web search looking for information on these styles, chances are the information you discover will vary from site to site. Therefore, you need to know the basics which are required to cite your sources.

The information listed below is an attempt to cover how to site the electronic sources not generally listed in the MLA or APA Style manuals. For general information on MLA and APA citations, the best sources are:

> Gibaldi, Joseph. *MLA Handbook for Writers of Research Papers.* 4th ed. NY:MLA, 1995.
> American Psychological Association. *Publication Manual of the American Psychological Association.* 4th ed. Washington, D. C.: APA, 1994.

When citing electronic sources, it is vital to type every letter, number, symbol, and space accurately. Any error can make it impossible to retrieve your source. Electronic sources tend to be transitory at best, which make them difficult to rely on, so besides insuring accuracy, printing a hard copy of sources you will cite will make it easier for you to cite accurately and provide evidence for your documentation. A current trend in documentation is to place angle brackets < > before and after internet addresses and URL's (Uniform Resource Locators). They have not been included here because as yet they are not widely used, but if you see them around an address you discover, be sure not to use them as part of the address when you attempt to retrieve a source.

Modern Language Association (MLA) Style Guidelines

These style guidelines follow the style sheets written for *Citations of Electronic Sources for MLA* written by Janice R. Walker of the University of Texas. Her Guidelines have been endorsed by the Alliance for Computers and Writing. Her guidelines can be reached at:

Modern Language Association (MLA)
http://www.cas.usf.edu/english/walker/mla.html

The MLA guidelines are also influenced by "MLA-Style Guidelines and Models for Documenting Internet Sources," by Andrew Harnack and Gene Kleppinger published in:

"Beyond the MLA Handbook: Documenting Sources on the Internet"
http://www.csc.eku.edu/honors/beyond-mla

In all instances of multiple authors, follow the standard MLA guidelines.

FTP (File Transfer Protocol) Sites

> Author's last name, Author's first name [if known]. "The Full Title of the Document [In quotation marks, following MLA standards for capitalization]." Date of publication [if available]. The abbreviation ftp [not followed by a period] the address of the ftp site and the full path to find the paper [not followed by a period] (the date of access in parentheses) [followed by a period].

Example:

> Kehoe, Brendan. "Zen and the Art of the Internet: A Beginner's Guide to the Internet." February 1992. ftp ftp.internic.net,pub/Internet-doc/zen.txt (March 26, 1997).

World Wide Web Sites (WWW)

> Author's last name, Author's first name [if known]. "The Full Title of the Document [In quotation marks, following MLA standards for capitalization]." *The Title of the Complete Work* [in italics, if applicable]. Date of publication or last revision [if available]. The address of the web site and the full path to find the paper [this is the URL, not followed by a period] [the URL may be included in angle brackets depending on the source] (the date of access in parentheses) [followed by a period].

Example:

> Harnack, Andrew and Gene Kleppinger. "Beyond the MLA Handbook: Documenting Electronic Sources on the Internet." June 10, 1996. Http://www.ttu.edu/kairos/1.2/inbox/mal_archive.html (March 23, 1997).

Synchronous Communications (such as Moos, MUDs, and IRCs)

> The name of the speaker(s). The type of discussion [such as a personal interview or group discussion]. The address [if applicable, not followed by a period] (the date in parentheses) [followed by a period].

Example:

> Ghostly Presence. Group Discussion. telnet moo.du.org:8000/ 80anon/anonview/1 4036#focus (March 26, 1997).

Gopher Sites

Author's name or alias (if known). "Title of the Work or Document" [if shown, in quotation marks, following MLA standards for capitalization]. *Any Print Publication Information* [in italics, if available, followed by a period]. The document date or date of publication [if available, followed by a period]. The gopher search path followed to access the information , or the full URL [with no closing punctuation] and directions to access the publication [with no closing punctuation] (the date of visit in parentheses) [followed by a period].

Examples:

Banks, Vickie and Joe Byers. "EDTECH." gopher://ericyr.syr.edu:70/00/Listervs/EDTECH/README "Using WAIS to Search the ERIC Digests." November 6, 1996. Gopher://gopher.ed.gov/70/00/programs/ERIC/searches/about_WAIS

Listserv messages

Author's name or alias [if known, in reverse order]. Author's e-mail address [not followed by a period] "The Subject Line from the Posting" [in quotation marks, following MLA standards for capitalization]. The date of publication [followed by a period]. The address of the listserv [not followed by a period] (the date of access in parentheses) [followed by a period].

Example:

Miller, Bradley D. millerb_gate@aacrao.nche.edu "Transnational Professional Practice." March 25, 1997. distancelearning-scope@igc.org,.internet (March 29, 1997).

If citing a file archived in a listserv or Web address, Harnack and Kleppinger suggest including the following information after the publication date. They also suggest the use of angle brackets around addresses.

Author's name or alias [if known, in reverse order]. Author's e-mail address [not followed by a period] "The Subject Line from the Posting" [in quotation marks, following MLA standards for capitalization]. The date of publication [followed by a period]. The address of the listserv [not followed by a period] (the date of access in parentheses) [followed by a period]. The list address [not followed by a period] via the address for the list's archive [not followed by a period] (The date of access) [in parentheses, followed by a period].

Newsgroup (USENET) messages

Author's name or alias [if known, in reverse order]. Author's e-mail address [not followed by a period] "The Subject Line from the Posting" [in quotation marks, following MLA standards for capitalization]. The date of publication [followed by a period]. The name of the Newsgroup [not followed by a period] (the date of access in parentheses) [followed by a period].

Example:

Wikrent, Anthony. "Physical Economy." Online. Usenet. November 9, 1996. News:talk.politics.medicine (November 19, 1996).

E-mail messages

Author's name or alias [if known, in reverse order]. Author's e-mail address [not followed by a period] "The Subject Line from the Posting" [in quotation marks, following MLA standards for capitalization]. The date of publication [followed by a period]. The kind of communication, such as personal, distribution list, office communication [followed by a period]. (The date of access in parentheses) [followed by a period].

Example:

Thonrton, Joe. JoeStage@aol.com "Using Computers." March 18, 1997. Personal. (March 19, 1997).

American Psychological Association (APA) Style Guidelines

The most recent edition of the *Publication Manual of the American Psychological Association* (4th Edition) does not include a definitive method for how the APA wants electronic sources to be documented; however, the web page for the American Psychological Association has published new guidelines for citing information from the World Wide Web. Go to:

http://www.apa.org/journals/webref.html

The general guidelines for these sources are to document them the same as other sources giving credit to the author and title and including the date of publication. Because of the transitory nature of the web, when doing research which will be documented in APA style, consider only using materials which can also be located in print sources, such as scholarly journals. When you do cite an electronic source, include as much information as possible to allow your reader to be able to retrieve the information. Any correspondence style communication should be documented within the body of your writing like personal communication, but you are not required to include it on your reference list. This would include references to e-mail, listservs, newsgroups, internet relay chats (IRCs), MOO's, or MUD's. Some sources do suggest their inclusion in your reference list, but this is not currently endorsed by APA.

According to "How to Cite Information From the World Wide Web" which is a link to the web site for the American Psychological Association:

> "All references begin with the same information that would be provided for a printed source (or as much of that information as possible). The web information is then placed at the end of the reference. It is important to use the "Retrieved from" and the date because documents on the Web may change in content, move, or be removed from a site altogether. . . . To cite a Web site in text (but not a specific document), it's sufficient to give the address (e.g., http://www.apa.org) there. No reference entry is needed." (http://www.apa.org/journals/webref.html)

Use the following as a guide for including a source on your reference list:

> Name of author [if given]. (Publication date) [in parenthesis]. Title of the article [following APA guidelines for

capitalization]. Title of Periodical or electronic text [underlined]. Volume number and/or pages [if any]. Retrieved [include the date here]from the World Wide Web: [Include the URL here, and do not end with a period]

Example:

A journal article:

>Murray, B. (February 1996). Virtual classrooms draw cheers, fears. *APA Monitor*. Retrieved March 29, 1997 from the World Wide Web: http://www.apa.org/monitor/feb96/distanca.html

Example:

A newspaper article:

>Stack, P. (January 25, 1997). "Is There A HAL Out There? Author compares '2001' computer with today's." p. E1. Retrieved from the World Wide Web: http://www.sfgate.com/cgi-bin/chronicle/article.cgi?file=DD50487.DTL&directory=/chronicle/archive/1997/01/25

Appendix IV
Netiquette

In everything we do, we seem to need a set of rules. Some people would follow them out of common courtesy whether they were written down or not. Others wouldn't follow them just because they were written down, but for those of you who really want to know the accepted, expected, and polite way of navigating the internet, here's how.

Everyone knows the old aphorism, "When in Rome . . . ." That pretty much fits the internet. Netiquette is a social agreement which allows a diverse range of people and personalities to function effectively. If you always keep in mind that you are sending your messages to people rather than just into cyberspace or on to other computers, then you can keep grounded in the human world rather than the virtual world. Also, remember that the use of the network is a privilege, not a right. Unlawful or abusive conduct may result in your privileges being temporarily revoked. Also, illegal activities can be prosecuted. But basically, netiquette just helps keep you from embarrassing yourself.

Netiquette for E-mail

Writing e-mail is much like writing an old fashioned letter, except usually an e-mail message is briefer. If you keep in mind the standard conventions of letter writing, sending e-mail will be a snap.

- Start out by being sure to use the correct address for your intended recipient. This includes making sure that when you are replying to an e-mail which has been sent to you, that you reply to the person you want your message to go to instead of to a whole cc list.
- Also be sure that your e-mail return address is included and your subject is clearly defined in the subject section. Never leave the subject blank, and don't make it too long so that the whole content can not be seen.

- Use a standard salutation depending on your audience, from Hi! to Dear Professor Smith.
- Be sure your message is brief, concise, and polite. If you need to send a long message, either attach a file or indicate that the message will be long right at the start.
- If you send encoded messages, be sure your recipient can unencode.
- Don't attach files longer than 50 kilobytes.
- Focus on one subject per message.
- Not all e-mail message systems have automatic word wrapping features, so get into the habit of automatically hitting the hard return or enter key after every 65-70 characters. If you don't, parts of your messages may be missing when they are received.
- Never give out your user ID or password. Also, it is safest to not disclose your home address, phone number, or place of business. Sending a pict file of yourself is also not a good idea.
- Don't assume anything you mail is private. It may show up archived somewhere on the net, it may be read by a systems administrator or your supervisor, a hacker might discover it, or you might accidentally send it to the wrong address.
- Use regular mixed case in your writing. Don't type in all capitals, referred to as shouting. Don't use excessive exclamation points, referred to as bangs. Use *asterisks* to show emphasis, and use a line at the beginning and end of something you want to _underline_.
- Don't be overly concerned about errors, yours or someone else's.
- Don't assume that because you mailed something to someone that it will be read or responded to.
- Respect copyrights.
- Don't get involved in chain letters.
- E-mail seems to be instant because when you click send, it is gone. But that doesn't mean that your recipients get it right away. They might, but it also might be hours or even days before your messages make it through the internet system. Be patient.
- Always say goodbye in some manner.
- You may wish to include a signature file with your messages. Be sure always to include at least your name and e-mail

address, and you may want to include your position and business. Besides that, don't go over four lines.

Netiquette for Listservs and Newsgroups

- All regular e-mail rules apply for listservs and newsgroups.
- When you sign up for a list, save your subscription letter so you know how to unsubscribe.
- Before you post to a listserv or newsgroup, lurk (observe) the group for awhile or read its archived messages so that you have an understanding of the group's ideology.
- Read the FAQs (frequently asked questions) or "Read Me" files before you post.
- Be sure any messages you post are related to the group topic.
- Delivery receipts are an invasion of privacy; don't use them
- If you have a disagreement with a person in the group, discuss in private e-mail, not distributed to the group.
- Avoid going on tangents or expressing pet peeves.
- Get permission from authors you quote before you quote them.
- Do not become involved in spamming (repeated posting of the same message to a newsgroup) or flaming (sending verbal electronic attacks). Remember, everyone looks at things differently.
- Write clear, brief subject lines and include only one subject per message. Make your message brief.
- Refer to URLs when available instead of sending large files to newsgroups.
- Don't send "test" messages.
- Make allowances for the cultural diversity of the group.
- Tolerate newbies (newcomers to the group or the internet culture).
- If you accidentally post something that is incorrect or that may be considered offensive, apologize right away.
- Quote enough of the message you are responding to for your message to be clear.
- Don't forward personal e-mail to newsgroups or listservs without permission.
- Don't say anything you don't want the whole world to know.
- Avoid sarcasm; readers can't tell your tone of voice.

- Don't post messages that just say "me too," " I don't know," " ditto," or "OK."
- Don't advertise.
- Don't cross-post, and post only to appropriate groups.
- Don't comment on spelling, grammar, and punctuation of other posters.
- Don't request help without including specific information.

Smileys

Smileys are used to help express emotion in writing. The meaning of smileys varies depending on who defines them, so use them sparingly and only when you are sure that their meaning won't be misinterpreted.

: -)	basic smiley, may be used to show happiness or sarcasm
; -)	winky, flirtatious or sarcastic
: -(	frowning, sad or depressed
: -I	indifferent
8-)	smiley with glasses or sunglasses
(-:	Left handed smiley
% -)	user has been at the computer too long
:'-(	user is crying
:-@	a scream
:-D	a laugh
:-*	a kiss

Acronyms

These acronyms and many more are kind of a shorthand for e-mail messages. As with smileys, only use them when you're sure your audience will understand what you are trying to express.

ADN	any day now
B4N	bye for now
BCNU	be seeing you
BTW	by the way
CU	see you
FC	fingers crossed
FWIW	for what it's worth
FYI	for your information
HTH	hope that helps

IC	I see
ILY	I love you
IMO	in my opinion
IMHO	in my humble opinion
IOW	in other words
LOL	laughing out loud
OBO	or best offer
ROFL	rolling on floor laughing
RTFM	read the funny manual
TIA	thanks in advance

URLs for Netiquette

"The Net: User Guidelines and Netiquette" by Arlene Rinaldi
http://www.vir.com/neti/index.html

Widely Used Smileys
http://www.nova.edu/Inter-Links/bigdummy/eeg_288.html#SEC289

Glossary
Fasten Your Seatbelts
Supercalifragilistics

And a technological extension of our bodies designed to alleviate physical stress can bring on psychic stress that may be much worse.

ActiveX This is a resource developed by Microsoft to extend the function of their *Internet Explorer* software.

Archie This is a search tool used to find resources that are stored on Internet-based FTP servers. Archie is short for Archive because it performs an archive search for resources. (See *FTP* and *Server*.)

AVI This stands for Audio/Video Interleaved. It is a Microsoft Corporation format for encoding video and audio for digital transmission.

Background This refers to an image or color that is present in the background of a viewed Web document. Complex images are becoming very popular as backgrounds but require a great deal more time to download. The color of the default background can be set for most Web browsers.

Bookmark This refers to a list of URLs saved within a browser. The user can edit and modify the bookmark list to add and delete URLs as the user's interests change. *Bookmark* is a term used by Netscape to refer to the user's list of URLs; *Hotlist* is used in *Mosaic* for the same purpose. (See *Hotlist*, *Mosaic*, and *URL*.)

Browser This is a software program that is used to view and browse information on the Internet. Browsers are also referred to as clients. (See *Client*.)

Bulletin Board Service   This is an electronic bulletin board. It is sometimes referred to as a BBS. Information on a BBS is posted to a computer where people can access, read, and comment on it. A BBS may or may not be connected to the Internet. Some are accessible by modem dial-in only.

Cache   This refers to a section of memory that is set aside to store information that is frequently used by the computer. Most browsers will create a cache for commonly accessed images. An example might be the images appearing in the user's homepage. Retrieving images from the cache is much quicker than downloading the images from the original source each time they are required.

Chat room   This is a site that allows real-time, person-to-person interactions.

Clickable image (Clickable map)   This refers to an interface used in Web documents that allow the user to click, or select, different areas of an image and receive different responses. Clickable images are becoming a popular way to offer a user many different selections within a common visual format.

Client   This is a software program used to view information from remote computers. Clients function in a Client-Server information exchange model. This term may also be loosely applied to the computer that is used to request information from the server. (See *Server*.)

Compressed file   This refers to a file or document that has been compacted to save memory space so that it can be easily and quickly transferred through the Internet.

Download   This is the process of transferring a file, document, or program from a remote computer to a local computer. (See *Upload*.)

E-mail   This is the short name for electronic mail. E-mail is sent electronically from one person to one or many other people. Some companies have e-mail systems that are not part of the Internet.

FAQ   This stands for Frequently Asked Questions. A FAQ is a file or document in which a moderator or administrator will post commonly asked questions and their answers. If you have a question, you should check for the answer in a FAQ first.

Forms This refers to an interface element used within Web documents to allow the user to send information back to a Web server. With a forms interface, the user is requested to type responses within entry windows to be returned to the server for processing. Forms rely on a server computer to process the submittals. They are becoming more common as browser and server software improve.

FTP This stands for *File Transfer Protocol*. It is a procedure used to transfer large files and programs from one computer to another. Access to the computer to transfer files may or may not require a password. Some FTP servers are set up to allow public access by anonymous logon. This process is referred to as *Anonymous FTP*.

GIF This stands for Graphics Interchange Format. It is a format created by CompuServe to allow electronic transfer of digital images. GIF files are a commonly-used format and can be viewed by both Macintosh and *Windows* users.

Gopher This is a format structure and resource for providing information on the Internet. It was created at the University of Minnesota.

GUI This is an acronym for Graphical User Interface. It is a combination of the appearance and the method of interacting with a computer. A GUI requires the use of a mouse to select commands on an icon-based monitor. Macintosh and *Windows* operating systems use GUIs.

Helper This is software that is used to help a browser view information formats that it couldn't normally view.

Homepage This refers to a Web document that a browser loads as a point of departure to browse the Internet. It also refers to a Web page maintained by an individual. In the most general sense, it is used to refer to any Web document.

Hotlist This is a list of URLs saved within the *Mosaic* Web browser. This same list is referred to as a *Bookmark* within the Netscape Web browser.

HTML   An abbreviation for HyperText Markup Language, the common language used to write documents that appear on the World Wide Web.

HTTP   An abbreviation for HyperText Transport Protocol, the common protocol used to communicate between World Wide Web servers.

Hypertext   This refers to text elements within a document that have an embedded connection to another item. Web documents use hypertext links to access documents, images, sounds, and video files from the Internet.

Inline image   This refers to images that are viewed along with text on Web documents. All inline images are in the GIF format. JPEG format is the other common image format for Web documents; an external viewer is typically required to view JPEG documents.

Java   This is an object-oriented programming language developed by Sun Microsystems.

JavaScript   This is a scripting language developed by Netscape in cooperation with Sun Microsystems to add functionality to the basic Web page. It is not as powerful as *Java* and works primarily from the client side.

JPEG   This stands for Joint Photographic Experts Group. It is also commonly used to refer to a format used to transfer digital images. (See *Inline image*.)

Jughead   This is a service for performing searches on the Internet. (See *Archie* and *VERONICA*.)

Mosaic   This is the name of the browser that was created at the National Center for Supercomputing Applications. It was the first Web browser to have a consistent interface for the Macintosh, Windows, and UNIX environments. The success of this browser is responsible for the expansion of the Web.

MPEG   This stands for Motion Picture Experts Group. It is also a format used to make, view, and transfer both digital audio and digital video files.

Newsgroup   This is the name for the discussion groups that can be on the *Usenet*. Not all newsgroups are accessible through the Internet. Some are accessible only through a modem connection. (See *Usenet*.)

Plug-in   This is a resource that is added to the Netscape *Navigator* to extend its basic function.

QuickTime   This is a format used by Apple Computer to make, view, edit, and send digital audio and video.

Server   This is a software program used to provide or serve information to remote computers. Servers function in a Client-Server information exchange model. This term may also be loosely applied to the computer that is used to serve the information. (See *Client*.)

Table   This refers to a specific formatting element found in HTML pages. Tables are used on HTML documents to visually organize information.

Telnet   This is the process of remotely connecting and using a computer at a distant location.

Upload   This is the process of moving or transferring a document, file, or program from one computer to another computer.

URL   This is an abbreviation for Universal Resource Locator. It is an address used by people on the Internet to locate documents. URLs specify the protocol for information transfer, the host computer address, the path to the desired file, and the name of the file requested.

Usenet   This is a world-wide system of discussion groups, also called newsgroups. There are many thousands of newsgroups, but only a percentage of these are accessible from the Internet.

VERONICA   This stands for *Very Easy Rodent-Oriented Netwide Index to Computerized Archives*. This is a database of menu names from a large number of Gopher servers. It is a quick and easy way to search Gopher resources for information by keyword. It was developed at the University of Nevada.

VRML This stands for Virtual Reality Markup Language. It was developed to allow the creation of virtual reality worlds. Your browser may need a specific plug-in to view VRML pages.

WAIS This stands for Wide Area Information Servers. This is a software package that allows the searching of large indices of information on the Internet.

WAV This stands for Waveform sound format. It is a Microsoft Corporation format for encoding sound files.

Web (WWW) This stands for the World Wide Web. When loosely applied, this term refers to the Internet and all of its associated elements, including Gopher, FTP, HTTP, and others. More specifically, this term refers to a subset of the servers on the Internet that use HTTP to transfer hyperlinked document in a page-like format.

The Easiest Way to Improve Your Writing!

NEW!
Writer's Helper
for Windows® and Macintosh®
3.5" Discs, Version 4.0

NOTHING CLARIFIES AND SIMPLIFIES AN IDEA LIKE THE RIGHT WORDS. Whether you're choosing, organizing, or revising your words, **WRITER'S HELPER V. 4.0** will help you communicate your ideas. From classroom writing assignments to memos, formal reports, business writing, and more, this software helps you convey your thoughts with a clear, concise style. From pre-writing to drafting to revising, **WRITER'S HELPER V. 4.0** guides you with interactive exercises and feedback through all phases of the writing process.

New Features of Version 4.0:
* New "exploration" activities to inspire ideas for writing.
* A new section on business writing (memos, reports, etc.).
* 2 new word check lists; 100 most commonly used words & common clichés.
* New "editor" to help customize activities such as word checks and writing prompts.
* Support for the newest version of WORDPERFECT® FOR WINDOWS 6.1 and MICROSOFT WORD® FOR WINDOWS '95.

Writer's Helper, Version 4.0 Minimum System Requirements
Windows®: An IBM® PC, PS/2 or 100% compatible computer with 1MB of free memory, 286 or better microprocessor, hard drive with 450K of free disk space, DOS Version 3.1 or later, and 3.5" Floppy drive (for installation). *Printer and color monitor recommended.*
Macintosh®: System with '020 or better processor, 4MB of RAM, hard drive with 450K of free disk space, 3.5-inch floppy drive for installation. *Printer and color monitor recommended.*

WINDOWS '95 AND 3.1 COMPATIBLE (0-13-615254-6) $18.00 net
MACINTOSH COMPATIBLE (0-13-615014-4) $18.00 net

TO ORDER YOUR COPY, please call 1-800-374-1200.
FOR SITE LICENSE INFORMATION, contact Rob Mejia,
Senior English Marketing Manager at rob_mejia@prenhall.com

PRENTICE HALL
One Lake Street, Upper Saddle River, NJ 07458

MAKE THE COMPUTER CONNECTION!

NEW WAYS OF WRITING: A HANDBOOK FOR WRITING WITH COMPUTERS
A Blair Press Book
SUSAN MILLER AND KYLE KNOWLES,
both of the University of Utah

This brief, spiralbound reference guide helps both the computer literate and the computer novice craft better writing and covers a wide range of writing situations at the computer. Visit the Miller/Knowles website at http://www.prenhall.com/miller
© 1997, 224 pp., paper (0-13-531260-4)

THE RESEARCH PAPER AND THE WORLD WIDE WEB: A WRITER'S GUIDE
DAWN RODRIGUES, *University of Texas—Brownsville*

This state-of-the-art text on Web searching provides students with strategies for researching on the Internet. It provides starting points for finding local and world-wide resources on the Internet; and suggests ways to organize all the information once gathered. Visit the Rodrigues website at http://www.prenhall.com/rodrigues
© 1997, 256 pp., paper (0-13-461724-X)

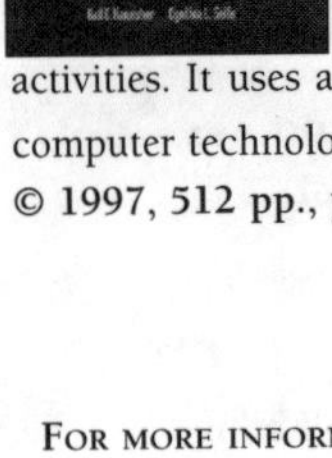

LITERACY, TECHNOLOGY, AND SOCIETY: CONFRONTING THE ISSUES
GAIL E. HAWISHER, *University of Illinois—Urbana-Champaign*
CYNTHIA L. SELFE, *Michigan Technological University*

Designed to help students become critical thinkers about technology, this reader engages students in a variety of reading, writing, and thinking activities. It uses a relatively non-technical approach to explore the various issues surrounding computer technology. Visit the Hawisher website at http://www.prenhall.com/hawisher
© 1997, 512 pp., paper (0-13-227588-0)

To order your copy, please call 1-800-374-1200.
For more information about these and other Prentice Hall titles, visit our online catalog at
http://www.prenhall.com